$Ch \ 2,3,4,5,6,7,8,$

ESSENTIALS
of CRIMINAL JUSTICE
and CRIMINOLOGY RESEARCH

Explanations and Exercises

James R. Lasley
Department of Criminal Justice
California State University, Fullerton

Prentice Hall
Upper Saddle River, NJ 07458

Acquisitions Editor: Neil Marquardt
Director of Production and Manufacturing: Bruce Johnson
Managing Editor: Mary Carnis
Marketing Manager: Frank Mortimer., Jr.
Editorial/Production Supervision and Interior Design:
    Inkwell Publishing Services
Cover Design: Miguel Ortiz
Manufacturing Buyer: Edward O'Dougherty

Printed in the United States of America
10 9 8 7 6 5 4 3 2 1

ISBN 0-13-080899-7

Prentice-Hall International (UK) Limited, *London*
Prentice-Hall of Australia Pty. Limited, *Sydney*
Prentice-Hall Canada Inc., *Toronto*
Prentice-Hall Hispanoamericana, S.A., *Mexico*
Prentice-Hall of India Private Limited, *New Delhi*
Prentice-Hall of Japan, Inc., *Tokyo*
Prentice-Hall of Southeast Asia Pte. Ltd., *Singapore*
Editora Prentice-Hall do Brasil, Ltda., *Rio de Janeiro*

Contents

MODULE 1

The Scientific Method in Criminal Justice Research   *1*

MODULE 2

Applied vs. Basic Criminal Justice Research   *13*

MODULE 3

Library Resources and Literature in Criminal Justice   *25*

MODULE 4

Putting the Scientific Method into Action   *41*

MODULE 5

Research Designs   *53*

CONTENTS

MODULE 6

The Criminal Justice Experiment   63

MODULE 7

Quasi-Experiments and Time Series   81

MODULE 8

The Criminal Justice Nonexperiment   95

MODULE 9

Surveys, Part I: Asking Questions about Criminal Justice Issues   *109*

MODULE 10

Surveys, Part II: Providing Answers to Survey Questions   *123*

MODULE 11

Surveys, Part III: Putting Criminal Justice Surveys Together   *135*

MODULE 12

Surveys, Part IV: Completing and Distributing Surveys *147*

MODULE 13

Sampling *159*

MODULE 14

Conducting Ethical Criminal Justice Research *173*

Research Abstracts   *185*

Index   *189*

Preface

During the middle of a research presentation to the Los Angeles Police Department, the Chief of Police interrupted me and said, "If I can't understand where those numbers came from, I'm not going to believe a word you say." At that point, he made me realize that there is a need to create some sort of research resource in the fields of criminal justice and criminology that helps anyone and everyone to "understand where those numbers came from." This book is the resource.

The point of this book is to help its reader become an informed consumer of research focusing on criminal justice and criminology issues. It contains what I believe to be the *essentials* of leading criminal justice and criminology research texts, with the exception of their drawn-out explanations or hard-to-understand technical talk. Instead, my goal is to provide you with clear, to-the-point descriptions and illustrations of everything you need to know in determining the strengths and weaknesses of criminal justice and criminology research.

The book's exercises, which are included at the end of each research module are designed to convey a "hands-on" understanding of each research essential through assignments such as the analysis of research abstracts and on-site library projects. In addition, all exercises were created to complement the content of existing research texts; or to be used as free-standing assignments.

JAMES R. LASLEY, PH.D.
Hollywood, California

MODULE 1

The Scientific Method in Criminal Justice Research

MODULE

LEARNING OBJECTIVE

To identify the key elements of the **scientific method** and to understand why it is an important tool for determining causes of and solutions to problems affecting the criminal justice system.

KEY LEARNING POINTS

THE SCIENTIFIC METHOD

The **scientific method** consists of the following key elements:

- Problem Identification
- Theory Building
- Hypothesis Formation
- Hypothesis Testing
- Specific and General Conclusions

PROBLEM IDENTIFICATION

It is essential that the problem is clearly identified at the beginning of the scientific method. The problem must be important, and it must not already have been solved. Ask yourself, "What is the exact problem?" to try to focus on the central issue. The key word is *focus*. Remember, there are usually many small problems that make up a big one. What we are concerned with here is the big problem and how to solve it.

THEORY BUILDING

If there is a recognizable problem, you must have some ideas about what is causing it or how to solve it. These educated guesses are called **theories**. Theories are really your best guess at why or how something is taking place. Theories are the most important part of the scientific method because they provide the clues for finding an answer to the problem. You will use the scientific method to test these clues and determine which are right and which are wrong.

HYPOTHESIS FORMATION

A hypothesis is simply an if-then statement that spells out one or more of the clues suggested by the theory. For example, suppose we want to test the theory that "street gangs are the product of bad schools." To turn this theory into a hypothesis we would say something like, "**If** schools in a neighborhood are bad **then** those neighborhoods are more likely to have street gangs." A single theory can generate many hypotheses. We could easily add more hypotheses to our sample theory such as, "**If** students' grades are low **then** the students are more likely to become gang members," or "**If** truancy rates are high in a particular school **then** it is more likely that gang involvement in that school will be high." A theory can have many possible twists or angles, and each of these can be used to form a separate hypothesis.

HYPOTHESIS TESTING

We test each separate hypothesis using a systematic evaluation method. In most cases, this will involve using some sort of **statistic**. Statistics are simply mathematical tools that allow us to determine the probability of being right or being wrong when we say a hypothesis is true or false. Sometimes we can use nonstatistical methods for evaluating hypotheses. Most of these methods involve scientific observation. In certain situations, it is possible to test a hypothesis by carefully observing and documenting the behavior of people or things.

SPECIFIC AND GENERAL CONCLUSIONS

Last, we have to identify likely answers to the problem we started with. These answers will be based on the results of your hypothesis testing. **Specific conclusions** are based on individual hypotheses. The **general conclusion** is based on an overall analysis of all hypotheses. It provides the big picture, combining the results of hypotheses that are true and those that are false. Don't ever be discouraged to find that all of your hypotheses are false. Often, this finding is more valuable than discovering that all of your hypotheses are true.

A NOTE ON RESEARCH OBJECTIVITY

The primary benefit of using the scientific method to perform criminal justice research is to ensure the **objectivity** of your research findings. In other words, by properly following the scientific method, you virtually guarantee that your research findings will be free from biases or influences that may distort the truth about what you are investigating. Remember that in criminal justice research as elsewhere, what you see is not always what you get. Very often, there are factors that we do not see or anticipate that influence our research findings. The scientific method helps us to detect and reveal these factors so we can report the most accurate and truthful findings about what we are attempting to study.

EXERCISES

MULTIPLE CHOICE TEST: SCIENTIFIC METHOD

Read each statement carefully, then choose the word or phrase that correctly completes the statement.

1. The method used by criminal justice researchers to investigate the causes of and solutions to crime-related issues is called
   a. the investigative method
   b. the scientific method
   c. the theoretical method
   d. the objective model   _____

2. The first step that must be carried out when using the scientific method is
   a. theory development
   b. hypothesis formulation
   c. problem identification
   d. hypothesis testing   _____

3. A theory is a (an)
   a. educated guess
   b. if-then statement
   c. statistical test
   d. research conclusion   _____

4. The statement, "*If* more police are hired *then* more crimes will be reported," is an example of a
   a. research problem
   b. research hypothesis
   c. research theory
   d. research conclusion   _____

5. Methods for testing research hypotheses, both scientific and nonscientific, include
   a. statistics
   b. nonstatistical methods

   c. observation

   d. all of these   _____

6. Statements made about the results of hypothesis tests are called

   a. formulated hypotheses

   b. specific conclusions

   c. general conclusions

   d. both b and c   _____

7. Which of the following is *not* a key element of the scientific method?

   a. personal opinion

   b. theory building

   c. hypothesis formulation

   d. problem identification   _____

8. The number of hypotheses that can be formulated for each theory is

   a. one

   b. two

   c. three

   d. many   _____

9. Which of the following steps in the scientific method comes directly before hypothesis testing?

   a. theory building

   b. problem identification

   c. hypothesis formulation

   d. conclusions   _____

10. The primary goal of the scientific method is to make sure that research findings are

   a. accurate

   b. objective

   c. interesting

   d. both a and b   _____

IDENTIFICATION MATCH: SCIENTIFIC METHOD

Each of the following statements describes an element of the scientific method. Using the key provided, match each statement with the correct element of the scientific method.

Key:
PI = problem identification
TB = theory building
HF = hypothesis formulation
HT = hypothesis testing
CO = general and specific conclusions

_____ 1. Although no formal studies have yet been done, the F.B.I. suspects that falling crime rates in the U.S. are the result of more states passing laws that are tough on criminals.

_____ 2. If white-collar offenders are given longer sentences for their crimes, then fewer corporate executives will steal from the companies that employ them.

_____ 3. The Uniform Crime Reports show that the number of violent female offenders has been increasing steadily over the past ten years.

_____ 4. According to recent statistical sources, the odds are that if children begin committing crimes at an early age then they will continue to commit crimes when they become adults.

_____ 5. Research findings suggest that citizens who feel that the police are their friends are more likely to report crimes; therefore, friendships between police and citizens created by community policing should increase the number of crimes reported to police.

_____ 6. The general idea of deterrence theory, that if the costs of crime exceed the benefits of crime then criminals will not act, has been supported by recent statistical research.

_____ 7. Researchers predict that a juvenile crime wave will hit the U.S. sometime in the next few years, based on population and age trends.

_____ 8. Correctional officials question the effectiveness of boot camps as a means for rehabilitating felons, because research findings show that recidivism rates for inmates assigned to boot camps are the same as for inmates serving time behind bars.

_____ 9. According to James Q. Wilson's Broken Windows Theory, if signs of urban decay such as graffiti and garbage are removed from high crime areas then crime in these areas should go down.

_____ 10. Research performed by Clarke suggests that all crime is specific to certain situations and that crime can be reduced by removing opportunities for criminals to commit crimes within these situations.

IS IT SCIENTIFIC OR NOT SCIENTIFIC?

For each statement, determine whether the source is scientific (i.e., discovered using the scientific method) or not scientific (i.e., discovered without using the scientific method).

1. A newspaper article reports an interview with a local police chief who claims that "drug abuse among teenagers is the result of coming from a broken home."
   a. scientific
   b. not scientific

2. Written decisions from a recent Supreme Court case report that ". . . the number of people who drink and drive will decrease if criminal sentences for drunk driving are made more severe."
   a. scientific
   b. not scientific

3. Surveys conducted with several hundred wardens indicate that the average number of prison riots in the U.S. has increased over the past year.
   a. scientific
   b. not scientific

4. The F.B.I. reports that the murder rate in many major U.S. cities has declined in past years, based on data provided to them from nearly every local police department in the nation.
   a. scientific
   b. not scientific

5. Officer X states that the true cause of juvenile delinquency is "too much sugar in the diets of young people," because every delinquent he has ever arrested has told him that he "eats lots of candy."
   a. scientific
   b. not scientific

MATCHING TEST: SCIENTIFIC METHOD

Insert the correct term or phrase after each definition.

scientific method   general conclusion
hypothesis testing   scientific observation
hypothesis formation   theory building
specific conclusion   problem identification
statistics   if-then question

1. A mathematical tool used to test a hypothesis

   _____

2. A research conclusion based on the test of an individual hypothesis

   _____

3. The process used to determine if theoretical clues are right or wrong

   _____

4. The proper format for expressing a hypothesis

_____

5. The starting point of the scientific method

_____

6. A research conclusion based on the tests of all hypotheses

_____

7. A nonstatistical method used to evaluate hypotheses

_____

8. An educated guess about the underlying causes of a research problem

_____

9. Creating specific if-then statements about a theory

_____

10. An examination of the truthfulness of hypotheses using statistics or nonscientific observation

_____

SHORT ANSWER TEST: SCIENTIFIC METHOD

Answer each of the following questions in the space provided.

1. How would you explain to a street cop who tells you "I've worked the streets for thirty years and I can spot criminals by the way they look" that he or she should use the scientific method (rather than just personal experience) to draw such a conclusion?

_____

_____

_____

_____

_____

_____

_____

_____

_____

2. What is meant by the term *objectivity* as it applies to the scientific method?

_____

_____

_____

_____

_____

_____

3. Apply the key steps of the scientific method to a criminal justice problem of your choice. The problem can be one you learned about in your studies, read about in the newspaper, or have experienced personally.

A. The Problem

_____

_____

_____

_____

_____

_____

B. The Theory

_____

_____

_____

_____

_____

_____

_____

_____

_____

C. Hypotheses (Supply at least three, written in if-then format.)

_____

_____

_____

_____

_____

_____

D. Conclusion (Assume all of your hypotheses are supported.)

_____

_____

_____

_____

_____

_____

2

Applied vs. Basic Criminal Justice Research

LEARNING OBJECTIVE

To identify the main conceptual and methodological differences between **applied** and **basic** criminal justice research.

KEY LEARNING POINTS

BASIC RESEARCH IN CRIMINAL JUSTICE

For criminal justice research to be classified as **basic**, it must address the basic or **root causes** of a particular problem or issue. Examples of basic research in criminal justice include studies that investigate the relationship between factors such as:

*   age and crime,
*   gender and crime,
*   lifestyle and risk of becoming a crime victim.

With regard to age and crime, we have discovered that people tend to age out of criminal behavior when they reach about 30 years of age. So, some of the root causes of criminal activity may be a product of youth. Likewise, we have found that the rate of criminal offending is many times higher among males than females; hence, some roots of crime may be socially or biologically linked to being male.

We have also found that being young and male increases your chances of becoming the victim of a personal or property crime. Many researchers have concluded that it is the lifestyle or routine activities that young males engage in that increase their risk of victimization. All of these studies have in common the goal of identifying **universal explanations** (i.e., explanations that explain all types of crime) rather than looking for specific explanations for specific crime situations.

APPLIED RESEARCH IN CRIMINAL JUSTICE

Applied research studies in criminal justice share in common the goal of investigating problems that are **symptoms** of the root cause. This is best explained by way of example. A recently emerging field of criminology called **Situational Crime Prevention** employs applied research methods and is based on the premise that the majority of crimes committed are the product of simple opportunity.

These researchers assume that when motivated criminals spot what they perceive to be an easy target (i.e., opportunity), they will strike. The key to stopping crime for criminologists who employ Situational Crime Prevention theory is to study a specific crime-prone situation and change it to reduce crime opportunities.

Recently, researchers in Great Britain had the opportunity to test the applied research ideas of Situational Crime Prevention on the problem of mob violence at soccer games. In London, many professional soccer games were being disrupted by mobs of angry fans breaking out in fights before the games even started. By studying the specific crime situation, researchers discovered that most of the fighting fans were riding buses to the games and arriving quite early. Before game time, they drank beer and started arguing, which often led to physical violence.

How would you change this situation to reduce criminal opportunity? The answer is simple: Change the bus schedule so the fans arrive only moments before the game; then they don't have the opportunity to drink and argue before the game starts. This is just what was done in London, and it worked!

EXERCISES

MULTIPLE CHOICE TEST: APPLIED VS. BASIC RESEARCH

Read each statement carefully, then choose the word or phrase that correctly completes the statement.

1. Criminal justice research that addresses the root causes of crime or criminal acts is called
   a. basic research
   b. applied research
   c. action research
   d. systematic research _____

2. The type of criminal justice research that focuses on the symptom of a particular problem or issue is known as
   a. basic research
   b. applied research
   c. action research
   d. systematic research _____

3. The primary goal of basic research in criminal justice is to search for
   a. specific causes
   b. symptoms
   c. universal explanations
   d. situational issues _____

4. Which of the following criminal justice research topics is *not* an example of basic criminal justice research?
   a. age and crime
   b. lifestyles and victimization
   c. situational crime prevention
   d. gender and crime _____

5. The criminal justice research finding that "people commit fewer crimes as they reach the age of 30 and beyond" is an example of
   a. basic research
   b. applied research

c. situational research

d. theoretical observation _____

IDENTIFICATION MATCH: APPLIED VS. BASIC RESEARCH

Each of the following statements describes an example of either basic or applied criminal justice research. Using the key provided, match each statement with the correct research example.

Key:
AP = applied criminal justice research
BA = basic criminal justice research

_____ 1. Crime statistics over the past several decades indicate that violent crimes are most likely to occur in the warmest summer months of July and August.

_____ 2. Research indicates that corporations that have few or no rules restricting their employees' behavior are more likely to fall victim to white-collar offending.

_____ 3. Many researchers claim that property crimes tend to increase when unemployment rates rise.

_____ 4. Males are most likely to be assaulted by other males, and females are most likely to be assaulted by males as well.

_____ 5. Gangs are less likely to engage in drive-by shootings on streets that have few avenues of escape.

_____ 6. Research indicates that most criminals tend to be generalists and commit a variety of criminal offenses.

_____ 7. It has been discovered that burglars are not likely to steal property that has been permanently marked with the owner's name.

_____ 8. Available data suggest that robberies are most likely to happen in streets and parking lots.

_____ 9. Statistics show that the majority of criminals tend to be under the age of 30, while evidence indicates that the majority of murderers tend to be older than the age of 30.

_____ 10. Social class appears to be a strong predictor of crime in research performed on crime data gathered by police.

MATCHING TEST: APPLIED VS. BASIC RESEARCH

Insert the correct term or phrase after each definition.

applied criminal justice research
basic criminal justice research
root cause
symptom
universal explanation
situational crime prevention
routine activities
age, gender, and social class

1. The focus of applied criminal justice research

_____

2. A method of applied criminal justice research

_____

3. Factors relating to crime discovered by basic criminal justice researchers

_____

4. Criminal justice research that explores the root causes of crime

_____

5. A factor discovered by basic criminal justice researchers to be linked to criminal victimization

_____

6. The desired result of basic criminal justice research

_____

7. Criminal justice research that focuses on the symptoms of crime and criminals

_____

8. The focus of basic criminal justice research

_____

SHORT ANSWER TEST: APPLIED VS. BASIC RESEARCH

Answer each of the following questions in the space provided.

1. What are the strengths and weaknesses of performing basic research studies on criminal justice problems or issues?

_____

_____

_____

_____

_____

_____

_____

_____

_____

_____

_____

_____

2. What are the strengths and weaknesses of performing applied research studies on criminal justice issues or problems?

_____

_____

_____

_____

_____

_____

_____

_____

3. Create a basic and applied criminal justice research study. For the basic study, identify the basic issue that you will investigate, how you might go about investigating the issue, and how the research findings may affect or change existing social policy. For the applied study, identify a crime situation and apply situational crime prevention to it. Be specific about how you would change the crime-prone situation to reduce criminal opportunity.

Basic Study:

_____

_____

_____

_____

_____

_____

_____

_____

_____

_____

_____

_____

NAME

_____

_____

_____

_____

_____

_____

_____

_____

_____

_____

_____

_____

_____

_____

_____

_____

_____

_____

_____

_____

_____

_____

Applied Study:

_____

_____

_____

_____

_____

NAME

Library Resources and Literature in Criminal Justice

LEARNING OBJECTIVE

To discover available academic and professional library resources in the field of criminal justice. To be able to identify the merit and quality of available criminal justice publications.

KEY LEARNING POINTS

ACADEMIC JOURNALS

The backbone of criminal justice research is the **academic journal.** These contain the most recent research findings in our field and they are much more timely than books. There are many different academic journals available that include research relating to criminal justice. However, the quality of the research reported in these journals varies greatly. Some journals are **peer reviewed** (meaning that they are evaluated for quality by experts in the field), while others are not. Some accept only a very few of the articles submitted to them; others accept a very high percentage of articles submitted. Generally speaking, the following journals include a large number of criminal justice research articles and employ a moderate to very rigorous review process:

- *Criminology*
- *Journal of Criminology and Criminal Law*
- *Justice Quarterly*
- *Crime and Delinquency*
- *Journal of Criminal Justice*
- *Law and Society Review*
- *Journal of Quantitative Criminology*
- *Police and Society*
- *Criminal Justice and Behavior*
- *Deviant Behavior*
- *Journal of Research in Crime and Delinquency*

In addition to these sources, many journals specific to other academic fields such as sociology, political science, psychology, or law (known as law reviews) contain useful information for criminal justice students.

THE PEER REVIEW PROCESS

Before a criminal justice research article appears in a particular peer reviewed journal, it must undergo a rigorous quality control process (i.e., the peer review process). This process involves many time-consuming steps. First, the author submits the article to a journal for blind review. This means that all information in the article that may suggest the author's identity (e.g., names and citations) is removed. Then the editor of the journal that the article has been submitted to sends the article to several (usually three or four) experts for their opinions on the article's

- research quality,
- timeliness,
- importance to the field of criminal justice,
- quality of writing and logic.

If the reviewers agree that the article makes a significant contribution to the field of criminal justice, the article is usually published. This process can take several months to a year or more if the reviewers suggest revisions to the article.

BOOKS

Unfortunately, many **books** in the field of criminal justice are dated before they are published, because it takes, on average, about one or two years for a book to become available after it is written. Books are great for theory building and historical development of a problem. They are not as good a resource for finding out the most cutting edge information regarding a topic. For that type of information, you need to go to the journals.

GOVERNMENT DOCUMENTS

Government documents are published by various local, state, and federal governmental agencies. They are often overlooked by criminal justice students, but can be a rich source of statistical studies and specialized data. Typically, government documents are not located on the shelves with books or other periodicals, but are placed in a central location in the library.

Federal documents are those published by the U.S. government. Most libraries group these documents under the call letter *J* (for Justice). Included among these sources are:

- *The Uniform Crime Reports* (published annually by the F.B.I.)
- *The National Crime Survey* (published annually by the D.O.J.)
- *Federal Probation* (published by the United States Courts)

Students of criminal justice should never overlook the *Sourcebook of Criminal Justice Statistics,* which is published annually by the Bureau of Justice Statistics. This document includes literally every statistic on every justice-related issue from local, state, and federal agencies. You should also look for special research reports published by the National Institute of Justice. The *Research In-Brief* series is especially useful for identifying quick summaries of state-of-the-art criminal justice research that is being performed within the United States.

Finally, don't forget state and local government documents, which are usually located near the federal documents. Accident records for the state, offense data for the state (similar to the Federal *UCR*), state prison and parole data, and various other state-level information can be found within the state government documents section of the library.

TRADE JOURNALS

Trade journals are similar to magazines, and typically include articles on criminal justice topics that are written by practitioners (people working in the field). They are very good sources of ideas for papers. They can also be used as supporting documentation to research findings that you include in your research. However, because trade journals tend not to be peer reviewed, they are not good sources to support your arguments in a position or research paper. Think of trade journal articles as expressions of opinions rather than as tested scientific fact. Some of the more popular trade journals include:

- *Police Chief*
- *Corrections Magazine*
- *FBI Law Enforcement Journal*
- *The Journal of California Criminal Justice*

REFERENCE MATERIALS

Reference materials usually cannot be checked out of the library. However, for criminal justice students, many reference materials provide quick, easy answers that may otherwise take hours to find in a book or journal article. Typical reference materials in criminal justice include dictionaries and encyclopedias of police, corrections, and criminology. A very good starting point for any student researching a criminal justice topic is the *Encyclopedia of Criminal Justice,* which contains short descriptions and references on nearly every topic relating to this field of study, written by experts in their respective areas.

INDEXES

Indexes are the central source for finding the location of journal articles, books, and even popular articles on a given criminal justice topic. The following indexes are recommended:

1. General Criminal Justice: *The Social Science Index, Criminal Justice Index*
2. General Legal Topics: *The Index to Legal Periodicals*
3. Newspaper Articles: *Los Angeles Times Index, New York Times Index,* (or index for your local newspaper)
4. Popular Articles: *Index to Periodical Literature* or *Lexis/Nexis* (on computer)

CITATION FORMAT

When you use any library resource in your written research, you must document or cite that source (in other words, give credit to the original researcher). There are many methods of documentation or **citation** used in criminal justice research. Some of these are included in manuals of style for the American Psychological Association, MLA, Turabian, and so forth. The examples given here are in a generic style that is used in many criminal justice sources.

JOURNAL

(One author)
Klein, M.W. (1971) Offense specialization and versatility among juveniles. *British Journal of Criminology,* 24, 185–194.

(Two authors)
Messner, S.F. & Tardiff, K. (1986) Economic inequality and levels of homicide. *Criminology,* 24, 297–317.

(Three or more authors)
Lasley et al. (1997) Researching justice in Los Angeles. *Contemporary Justice*, 1, 1–35.

BOOK

Wycoff, M.A. (1982) *Role of the municipal police: Research as a prelude to changing it.* Washington, D.C.: Police Foundation.

CHAPTER IN EDITED BOOK

Easterman, Richard A. (1974) Does economics improve crime rates? In Helen Oretski and Robert Slagel (eds.), *What Is the Nature of Crime?* New York: Soquel Press.

GOVERNMENT DOCUMENT

Bureau of Justice Statistics. (1994) *Sourcebook of Criminal Justice Statistics–1993.* Washington, D.C.: U.S. Government Printing Office.

EXERCISES

MULTIPLE CHOICE TEST: LIBRARY RESOURCES

Read each statement carefully, then choose the word or phrase that correctly completes the statement.

1. The most recent criminal justice research findings are found in
   a. trade journals
   b. books
   c. government documents
   d. academic journals _____

2. Documents such as the *Uniform Crime Reports (UCR)* that contain specialized criminal justice statistics can be found in
   a. books
   b. academic journals
   c. government documents
   d. trade journals _____

3. Articles on criminal justice topics that are written by practitioners such as police, judges, and correctional officials can be found in
   a. academic journals
   b. trade journals
   c. government documents
   d. books _____

4. The library reference source used to locate journal articles, books, and popular articles on given criminal justice topics is called a (an)
   a. reference link
   b. index
   c. resource guide
   d. locator _____

5. The quality of criminal justice research included in academic journals is determined by

   a. editorial review

   b. periodic review

   c. peer review

   d. mutual review   _____

6. Specialized materials such as the *Encyclopedia of Criminal Justice* that cannot be checked out of the library are called

   a. trade journals

   b. government documents

   c. reference materials

   d. academic journals   _____

7. Sources for theory building and historical development of a criminal justice problem that tend to be dated before they come out are

   a. trade journals

   b. books

   c. government documents

   d. academic journals   _____

8. The *FBI Law Enforcement Journal* is an example of a (an)

   a. trade journal

   b. book

   c. government document

   d. academic journal   _____

9. *Law and Society Review* is an example of a (an)

   a. trade journal

   b. book

   c. government document

   d. academic journal   _____

10. Specialized formats used for documenting information used in research papers and reports are called

   a. indexes

   b. citations

   c. references

   d. summaries   _____

IDENTIFICATION MATCH: LIBRARY RESOURCES

Each of the following statements describes a criminal justice library resource. Using the key provided, match each statement with the correct library resource.

Key:
AJ = academic journal
BO = book
GD = government document
TJ = trade journal
RM = reference materials
IN = indexes

_____ 1. Contains up-to-date criminal justice research information, and is often peer reviewed.

_____ 2. Contains statistics from local, state, and federal law enforcement agencies.

_____ 3. Contains articles that tend not to be peer reviewed and that are written by persons working in the field of criminal justice.

_____ 4. Used to locate academic journal articles as well as newspaper articles relating to criminal justice issues and topics.

_____ 5. *Police Chief* and *Corrections Magazine* are examples.

_____ 6. *Justice Quarterly* is an example.

_____ 7. Includes resources such as dictionaries and encyclopedias related to criminal justice issues and topics.

_____ 8. Contains criminal justice information that tends to be dated (one or more years old) by the time it is published.

_____ 9. The *Social Science Index* is an example.

_____ 10. The *National Crime Survey* is an example.

IS THE CITATION CORRECT?

Identify whether each of the following citations is correct or incorrect according to the standard method of criminal justice citation included in this module.

1. *Academic Journal:*

   Clarke, R.V. (1992) *Situational Crime Prevention.* New York, NY: Springer-Verlag Publishers.

   a. correct   **b.** incorrect

2. *Academic Journal:*

   Lasley, J.R. (1989) Drinking routines/lifestyles and predatory victimization. *Justice Quarterly,* 6, 529–542.

   a. correct   **b.** incorrect

3. *Book:*

   Cressey, D.R. (1953) *Other People's Money.* Glencoe, Ill: The Free Press.

   a. correct   **b.** incorrect

4. *Book:*

   Felson, M. (1994) Crime and Everyday Life. Newbury Park, CA: Pine Forge.

   a. correct   **b.** incorrect

5. *Academic Journal (Two Authors):*

   Fowles, R. and Merva, M. (1996) Wage inequality and criminal activity. *Criminology,* 34, 163–182.

   a. correct   **b.** incorrect

MATCHING TEST: LIBRARY RESOURCES

Insert the correct term or phrase after each definition

reference materials	books
indexes	government documents
peer review	citation
trade journals	academic journals

1. Sources used to locate library materials

2. A method used to document research sources

_____

3. Documents containing recent research findings

_____

4. Documents containing local, state, or federal statistics

_____

5. Documents taking several years to publish

_____

6. Documents that cannot be checked out of the library

_____

7. The quality control process of published research

_____

8. Documents written by criminal justice practitioners

_____

SHORT ANSWER TEST: LIBRARY RESOURCES

Answer each of the following questions in the space provided.

1. Describe the peer review process. How does this process relate to the quality of research published in academic journals?

_____

_____

_____

_____

_____

_____

_____

_____

_____

_____

_____

_____

_____

_____

_____

_____

_____

_____

2. For the following sources, please write the correct citation format (for example, write your citation in journal format if the facts section says *journal;* write your citation in book format if the facts section says *book*).

A. Facts (Journal, 1 Author)

Author: J. R. Richardson
Title: Stopping Crime in the Suburbs
Date: 1997
Journal: Journal of Contemporary Crime
Issue: Volume 24
Pages: 234–267
Correct Citation Format:

_____

_____

_____

B. Facts (Journal, 2 Authors)

Authors: J.R. Smith & T.S. Rand
Title: Curbing Juvenile Drug Use
Date: 1987

Journal: Drug Addiction
Issue: Volume 12
Pages: 12–35
Correct Citation Format:

_____

_____

_____

C. *Facts (Journal, Multiple Authors)*

Authors: E. Lloyd, J.Q. Yepp, and J. Olin
Title: Designing Out Gangs
Date: 1989
Journal: Street Gangs
Issue: Volume 4
Pages: 345–378
Correct Citation Format:

_____

_____

_____

D. *Facts (Book)*

Author: J.Q. Evans
Title: Homicide in the Inner City
Date: 1990
Publisher: Criminal Justice Press, Chicago, Illinois
Correct Citation Format:

_____

_____

_____

E. *Facts (Chapter in Edited Book)*

Chapter Author: J. Roberts
Title/Book: Crime in the Year 2000

Book Editor: E.C. McKey
Publisher: New Press, New York, NY
Title/Chapter: Exploring Crime
Date: 1997
Correct Citation Format:

_____

_____

_____

F. Facts (Government Document)

Title: Official State Crime Statistics Report, 1996
Publisher: State Press
Publishing Agency: State Highway Patrol,
Sacramento, CA
Date: 1997
Correct Citation Format:

_____

_____

_____

3. Go to your university or college library and answer the following questions by locating each of the criminal justice library resources listed.

   a. Does your library have a federal government documents section? If so, where is it located?

   _____

   _____

   _____

   b. Does your library have a state government documents section? If so, where is it located?

   _____

   _____

   _____

   c. What are the call letters in your library for books on criminal justice topics?

_____

_____

_____

_____

   d. What are the call letters in your library for government documents in your state?

_____

_____

4. In your library locate an example of each of the following criminal justice resources and write down the call letters for each one.

Academic Journal

Title: _____

_____

Call Letters: _____

Criminal Justice Book

Title: _____

_____

Call Letters: _____

Criminal Justice Government Document (Federal, State or Local)

Title: _____

_____

Call Letters: _____

Criminal Justice Trade Journal

Title: _____

_____

Call Letters: _____

Criminal Justice Reference Material

Title: _____

_____

Call Letters: _____

Criminal Justice Index

Title: _____

_____

Call Letters: _____

4

Putting the Scientific Method into Action

To develop the ability to construct directional and nondirectional hypotheses. To understand the meaning of the terms independent and dependent variable. To be able to create clear operational definitions for research concepts and variables.

KEY LEARNING POINTS

INDEPENDENT AND DEPENDENT VARIABLES

Quite simply, a variable is anything that varies, changes, or has differences. Something that never changes is a constant. In criminal justice research we typically deal with two types of variables: independent and dependent. **Independent variables** are things that cause or effect change in some other variables. Simply put, they are the things that cause other things to change. **Dependent variables** are changed or affected by the independent variable. Independent variables always come before dependent variables in time and in space:

Independent Variable ——————> Dependent Variable

VARIABLE ATTRIBUTES

Attributes are characteristics of variables. For example, there could be several possible attributes to the variable, police officer:

- male officers and female officers,
- short officers and tall officers,
- rookie officers and veteran officers.

The above examples are just a few of the many attributes that could be used to describe the variable, police officer. Remember, all variables must have attributes; otherwise they would be constants rather than variables.

DIRECTIONAL HYPOTHESES AND RELATIONSHIPS

There are two types of hypotheses: directional and nondirectional. A **directional hypothesis** is one that specifies that a relationship between two variables moves in a given direction. This direction can be either **positive** or **negative** (also called **inverse**). For example, we may say that if Variable A increases then Variable B will increase. This is known as a positive relationship, because the independent and dependent variables are moving in the same direction.

On the other hand, we have a negative or inverse relationship if Variable A decreases when Variable B increases. Thus, directional hypotheses are called directional because they predict a specific direction in the relationship between a set of variables.

NONDIRECTIONAL HYPOTHESES

On the other hand, **nondirectional hypotheses** do not (and cannot) predict a specific direction between a set of variables. Instead, we word the hypothesis to indicate that we are uncertain how a change in Variable A will affect Variable B. Typical nondirectional hypotheses say something like, If Variable A increases then Variable B will change; or, There is a relationship between Variable A and Variable B; or, Variable

A affects Variable B. You will notice that the above examples do not specify a direction of change for Variable B. That is what all nondirectional hypotheses have in common.

When should you use a directional hypothesis versus a nondirectional hypothesis? The answer to this question lies in a complete literature review of your research problem. If there is sufficient research to suggest that Variable A will make Variable B go up or down, then you should write a directional hypothesis that indicates this relationship. We call this **confirmatory research**, because you are confirming a relationship that is hypothesized to exist in the real world.

Write nondirectional hypotheses when you are investigating a problem that is new or has received little previous scientific investigation. We call this **exploratory research**, because we are exploring an area that is, in a sense, uncharted ground. Remember, the basic goal of criminal justice research is to provide an honest, objective answer to a problem. If we were to go so far as to write a directional hypothesis about something that we know nothing about, we might be tempted to prove that hypothesis.

If we really don't know how Variable A affects Variable B, a nondirectional hypothesis that says basically, I don't know what Variable A will do to Variable B, keeps us honest.

OPERATIONAL DEFINITIONS

How the researcher defines variables for the purposes of a particular study is referred to as an **operational definition**. These definitions are very important for several reasons. First, they provide the reader of the research with a general idea of the boundaries or the limitations of the research. For example, suppose you read a research study reporting that "kids who eat Twinkies are 20 times more likely to commit crime than kids who do not eat Twinkies." Would you conclude that Twinkie eaters are robbers, rapists, and murderers? You might if you did not read the researcher's operational definition of the term *crime,* to discover that *crime* according to the researcher is limited to acts such as "fighting in the schoolyard" or "not obeying a teacher." The operational definition tells you exactly what the variable means.

Second, in many cases, research must be replicated to make sure that findings are accurate. The more times we can repeat a given research study and produce the same findings, the more certain we are that the conclusions of the researchers can be trusted. However, it is very difficult to replicate a study in a precise manner if we don't know precisely how the variables were defined or measured. So the operational definition is of vital importance to the researcher who wishes to replicate a study.

EXERCISES

MULTIPLE CHOICE TEST: SCIENTIFIC METHOD

Read each statement carefully, then choose the word or phrase that correctly completes the statement.

1. A variable that acts as the cause of another variable is called the
   a. dependent variable
   b. independent variable
   c. endogenous variable
   d. first factor _____

2. The specific definitions given by the researcher to variables used in a criminal justice research study are called
   a. independent variables
   b. variable attributes
   c. operational definitions
   d. dependent variables _____

3. Operational definitions make it easier for other criminal justice researchers to conduct a study
   a. sample
   b. replication
   c. observation
   d. examination _____

4. Characteristics of a variable are known as
   a. variable attributes
   b. independent variables
   c. dependent variables
   d. samples _____

5. Hypotheses predicting the direction of a relationship between variables are
   a. directional
   b. nondirectional
   c. operational
   d. attributive _____

6. The statement, "There is a relationship between a police officer's educational background and his or her performance on the job," is an example of a
   a. nondirectional hypothesis
   b. directional hypothesis
   c. variable attribute
   d. research query   _____

7. Directional hypotheses are used when conducting criminal justice research that is
   a. exploratory
   b. situational
   c. observational
   d. confirmatory   _____

8. When conducting research on a criminal justice topic that has never been investigated, the researcher should use hypotheses that are
   a. directional
   b. confirmatory
   c. sampled
   d. nondirectional   _____

9. A hypothesis that states, "If laws get tougher then the number of violent crimes will go down," is an example of a (an)
   a. positive relationship
   b. negative relationship
   c. inverse relationship
   d. null relationship   _____

10. The relationship between unemployment and crime is
    a. positive
    b. negative
    c. inverse
    d. both b and c   _____

IDENTIFICATION MATCH: SCIENTIFIC METHOD

Each of the following questions refers to either an independent or a dependent variable. Using the key provided, match each question with the correct variable type.

Key:
IV = independent variable
DV = dependent variable

_____ 1. If crime decreases as the result of decreases in street drug sales, then crime is what type of variable?

_____ 2. If it is discovered that the number of violent crimes increases as outdoor temperature increases, then outdoor temperature is what type of variable?

_____ 3. If research tells us that as people age they are less likely to commit crimes, then a person's age is what type of variable?

_____ 4. If juries are more likely to impose the death penalty on defendants who are in gangs, then the death penalty is what type of variable?

_____ 5. If research findings indicate that children are more likely to be criminal when their friends are criminal, then having or not having criminal friends is what type of variable?

_____ 6. If positive attitudes toward police increase as the result of increased communication between police and citizens, then increased communication between citizens and police is what type of variable?

_____ 7. If there is a cause and effect relationship between alcohol abuse and spousal abuse, then spousal abuse is what type of variable?

_____ 8. If a person's routine activities increase the chances of becoming the victim of a crime, then a person's routine activities are what type of variable?

_____ 9. If it is found that the number of homicides is linked to the number of handguns sold illegally, then the number of homicides is what type of variable?

_____ 10. If it is discovered that police are more likely to arrest a suspect who has a surly demeanor, then demeanor is what type of variable?

POSITIVE OR NEGATIVE RELATIONSHIPS?

For each of the variable pairs listed, indicate whether the relationship between the variables is likely to be positive or negative.

1. Illegal drug sales and drug abuse
   a. positive   b. negative
2. Unemployment and credit card fraud
   a. positive   b. negative
3. Gangs and drive-by shootings
   a. positive   b. negative
4. Car alarm sales and auto thefts
   a. positive   b. negative
5. Traffic officers and speeding citations
   a. positive   b. negative
6. Convenience stores and armed robberies
   a. positive   b. negative
7. Age and criminal victimization
   a. positive   b. negative
8. Vice detectives and prostitution
   a. positive   b. negative
9. Number of corporate executives and number of white-collar crimes
   a. positive   b. negative
10. Sobriety check points and drunk drivers
    a. positive   b. negative

MATCHING TEST: SCIENTIFIC METHOD

Insert the correct term or phrase after each definition.

independent variable	directional hypothesis
confirmatory research	variable attribute
dependent variable	operational definition
exploratory research	nondirectional hypothesis
negative relationship	positive relationship

1. As variable A increases, variable B decreases

2. A variable as defined by the researcher

3. What a robbery is to the variable crime

4. Research on unexplored criminal justice topics

5. A variable that causes another variable to change

6. A variable that changes as the result of another variable

7. A hypothesis used in exploratory research

8. Research that is based on directional hypotheses

9. As variable A increases, variable B increases

10. A relationship between variables A and B

SHORT ANSWER TEST: SCIENTIFIC METHOD

Answer each of the following questions in the space provided.

1. Under what conditions should criminal justice researchers use directional hypotheses rather than nondirectional hypotheses? Provide examples that relate to a criminal justice topic.

_____

_____

_____

_____

_____

_____

_____

_____

_____

_____

_____

_____

_____

_____

_____

_____

_____

_____

_____

_____

_____

2. Why are operational definitions important?

_____

_____

_____

_____

_____

3. What is meant by the term *independent variable*?

_____

_____

_____

_____

_____

4. What is meant by the term *dependent variable*?

_____

_____

_____

_____

_____

5. What is meant by the term *variable attribute*?

_____

_____

_____

_____

_____

_____

6. Construct five directional hypotheses that relate to a criminal justice topic.

a. _____

_____

b. _____

_____

c. _____

_____

d. _____

_____

e. _____

_____

7. Construct five nondirectional hypotheses that relate to a criminal justice topic.

a. _____

_____

b. _____

_____

c. _____

_____

d. _____

_____

e. _____

_____

Research Designs

LEARNING OBJECTIVE

To describe and understand the importance of research designs for carrying out the scientific method. To comprehend the importance of using research designs to ensure the validity and reliability of research findings.

KEY LEARNING POINTS

THE IMPORTANCE OF RESEARCH DESIGNS

The research design is the backbone of criminal justice research. A good research design provides the criminal justice researcher with a set of steps or rules that, when followed exactly, will ensure that the study's findings are accurate and can be trusted. In other words, the research design is a method of conducting studies that allows us to produce **reliable** and **valid** findings.

RELIABILITY AND VALIDITY

For a study to be accurate, its findings must be reliable and valid. Reliable findings are simply those that we can assume to be consistently the same if we were to do a particular study over and over again. For example, as you may already know, candidates for most criminal justice jobs must take and pass a written psychological exam before being hired. If X achieves a score of 100 on this exam, then takes the same test again and makes the same score of 100, we could say that X's score on the psychological test is a reliable one. In other words, the score didn't change between the first and second time X took the test.

Validity refers to the truthfulness of research findings. The main question criminal justice researchers must ask themselves when thinking about validity is, "Does this study really say what I think it says?" That is, for research findings to be valid, you must be sure your results indicate what you say they do. In the case of the psychological test, X may have a reliable score of 100, but does this score really measure X's psychological condition? Or does it measure something else, such as I.Q. or bank account balance? For the psychological test to be valid, we must be sure that X's score of 100 is measuring X's psychological condition and nothing else.

Later, we will discuss in detail how to conduct specific tests to discover if your research is reliable or valid. For now, you should know that research designs that are constructed properly will produce reliable and valid findings. One other important point to remember is that reliability always follows validity. That is, if you are sure that your study findings are valid, then you can be sure that they are also reliable. However, if your findings are reliable, you **can't** automatically assume that they are valid.

EXTRANEOUS VARIABLES

Research designs ensure certain levels of reliability and validity of research findings by screening out or blocking **extraneous variables**. Extraneous variables are unwanted effects that serve to contaminate a variable relationship that is being studied. For example, when we study the cause and effect relationship between two variables (say, A and B), we do not want the effects of other variables (say, X, Y, and Z) creeping into our study. If such extraneous effects do contaminate the relationship we are studying, we will never be sure whether it is our independent variable (i.e., A) that is affecting our dependent variable (i.e., B). This is so because extraneous variables that have crept into our study (i.e., X, Y, and Z) may be the ones affecting our dependent variable. The term **internal invalidity** refers to a research design that has become contaminated by the effects of extraneous variables.

TYPES OF RESEARCH DESIGN

The three types of research design are **experimental, quasi-experimental** and **nonexperimental** (sometimes called **correlational**). Although all of these types of designs are used in criminal justice research, quasi-experimental and nonexperimental designs are the most commonly used to research crime and justice issues. Although we will discuss each of these designs in greater detail within separate modules, a brief description of each is provided below:

- *Experiment:* The researcher assigns subjects at random to two groups. One group is called the control group; the other is called the experimental group. A treatment or change is introduced to the experimental group but is not introduced to the control group. Differences between the experimental and control groups are assumed to be caused by the treatment.

- *Quasi-experiment: Quasi* means *as if* or *almost.* Thus, the quasi-experiment is almost an experiment. It is almost an experiment because it does not contain a true control group, as an experiment does. Quasi-experimental designs are used primarily for evaluating before and after changes in criminal justice policies. For example, the effects of a new gun control law may be studied by comparing the number of arrests for carrying a concealed weapon before and after the passage of the law. There is no real control group used here, except the time period before the law was passed.

- *Nonexperiment:* This type of design does not involve the use of a control group. Most nonexperimental research is carried out in the form of surveys. Because surveys do not use treatments or control groups they can, at best, only predict the relationship between things. They use statistically equivalent groups to make these predictions.

THE POWER OF RESEARCH DESIGNS

The **power** of a research design refers to the design's ability to block out extraneous variables and to provide a true research finding. The more powerful the research design, the less likely it is that we will believe we have found a cause and effect relationship when in reality the relationship does not exist. Experiments are the most powerful of research designs. Quasi-experiments are second in power to experiments, and nonexperimental designs are the least powerful of the three types.

CROSS-SECTIONAL VS. LONGITUDINAL STUDIES

When selecting a particular research design, it is important to consider what time frame is most appropriate for your study. There are two time frames to choose from. Studies based on **cross-sectional** time frames are used when the researcher wants to describe a particular issue, situation, or thing, but is not concerned with determining cause and effect. Because cross-sectional studies look at things only in one place and only at one particular time, they do not provide the researcher with the ability to determine which things are causing each other.

Longitudinal studies, on the other hand, explore issues, situations, or things over two or more separate time periods and allow the researcher to make cause and effect conclusions. When we look at variables over several different time periods, we can tell whether changes we see are consistent over time and not just odd, random, or one-time changes that are caused by something other than what we are studying.

EXERCISES

MULTIPLE CHOICE TEST: RESEARCH DESIGNS

Read each statement carefully, then choose the word or phrase that correctly completes the statement.

1. Criminal justice research findings that are consistent from one study to the next are called
   a. valid
   b. objective
   c. reliable
   d. powerful   _____

2. Weak or ineffective criminal justice research designs will likely produce research findings that are
   a. trustworthy
   b. reliable
   c. valid
   d. invalid   _____

3. The ability of a research design to produce reliable and valid findings is called
   a. strength
   b. power
   c. resistance
   d. constructiveness   _____

4. Research designs that study a criminal justice event at one particular point in time are called
   a. cross-sectional
   b. panel
   c. targeted
   d. longitudinal   _____

5. Research designs that study a criminal justice event over a period of time are called
   a. cross-sectional
   b. panel
   c. targeted
   d. longitudinal   _____

6. Criminal justice research designs that involve true control groups created by random assignment are called
   a. experiments
   b. quasi-experiments
   c. nonexperiments
   d. qualitative   _____

7. Research designs that involve the creation of control groups designed by the researcher rather than created through random assignment are called
   a. experiments
   b. quasi-experiments
   c. nonexperiments
   d. qualitative   _____

8. Research designs that do not have control groups, but rely on statistical controls, are called
   a. experiments   c. nonexperiments
   b. quasi-experiments   d. qualitative   _____

9. If a criminal justice research design produces findings that measure what the study is intended to measure, these findings are considered
   a. valid   c. invalid
   b. reliable   d. both a and b   _____

10. Variables that are intended to be excluded or blocked out by a research design are called
    a. independent   c. extraneous
    b. dependent   d. powerful   _____

IDENTIFICATION MATCH: RESEARCH DESIGNS

Each of the following statements describes a criminal justice research design. Using the key provided, match each statement with the correct research design.

Key:
EX = experiment
QE = quasi-experiment
NE = nonexperiment

_____ 1. A research design that has a true control group

_____ 2. A research design that produces surveys

_____ 3. A research design that has no control group

_____ 4. A research design that uses a control group created by the researcher

_____ 5. The most powerful research design

_____ 6. The least powerful research design

_____ 7. A research design used to evaluate before and after results regarding criminal justice laws and programs

_____ 8. The most difficult, and rarely used, research design in studying criminal justice issues and problems

_____ 9. The research design used in the National Crime Survey

_____ 10. The second most powerful criminal justice research design

MATCHING TEST: RESEARCH DESIGNS

Insert the correct term or phrase after each definition.

reliability   extraneous variables
longitudinal   experiment
internal invalidity   quasi-experiment
cross-sectional   nonexperiment
power   validity

1. The ability of a research design to produce reliable and valid findings

   _____

2. A research design that is also called correlational

   _____

3. Something that is always assumed to exist when validity is present

   _____

4. A research design that involves random assignment

   _____

5. A research design that is almost experimental

   _____

6. A term describing a study that takes place over time

   _____

7. Factors that interfere with reliability and validity

   _____

8. A term that refers to contaminated research findings

_____

9. A term describing a study that takes place at one time only

_____

10. A term used to describe research findings that measure what they intend to measure

_____

SHORT ANSWER TEST: RESEARCH DESIGNS

Answer each of the following questions in the space provided.

1. Define the terms _reliability_ and _validity_. Provide an example of each using a criminal justice issue or topic.

_____

_____

_____

_____

_____

_____

_____

_____

_____

_____

2. What is the relationship between the power of a research design and its ability to produce findings that are reliable and valid?

_____

_____

_____

_____

_____

_____

_____

3. Go to the academic journal section in your library. Locate one article. Describe which type of research design is being used: experimental, quasi-experimental, or nonexperimental. Tell what evidence is available in the article that was helpful in your identification of the research design.

   Article Title:

_____

_____

   Research Design and Evidence:

_____

_____

_____

_____

_____

_____

_____

_____

The Criminal Justice Experiment

LEARNING OBJECTIVE

To gain a basic understanding of experimental design and to learn the steps necessary to carry out a basic experiment.

KEY LEARNING POINTS

COMPONENTS OF THE EXPERIMENT

All experiments, regardless of their size or complexity, are made up of common components. These include 1) random assignment, 2) the control group, 3) the experimental group, and 4) the treatment. The components and their specific importance to the experimental design are explained below.

RANDOM ASSIGNMENT

In criminal justice research, whether or not an experiment can or should be performed boils down to the issue of **random assignment.** Before even considering the use of an experiment, criminal justice researchers must ask themselves the following questions:

- Is it possible to separate the people or things you intend to study into groups?
- Can the people or things you intend to study be divided into groups at random?
- Can the process of randomly creating groups be done morally, ethically, legally, and without harming the people or things you intend to study?

Answering "no" to any of the above questions should send a warning to criminal justice researchers that the random assignment component of experimental design cannot be (or should not be) utilized.

Random assignment is the backbone of any experiment. Without it the data obtained from experiments are useless. Unfortunately, random assignment is especially difficult to perform in crime and justice research settings without increasing harm to or withholding services from experimental subjects. Unlike psychologists or biologists who perform carefully controlled experiments under ideal laboratory conditions, researchers in crime and justice use inner-city streets, prison cell blocks, and courtrooms as their labs.

Random assignment is carried out by separating the subjects of study into two or more groups, while ensuring that all subjects have an equal chance of being assigned to each group. If random assignment is performed correctly, we can assume that each group of subjects created will be *statistically equal* in all respects. For example, if a pool of 50 judges was separated at random into two groups consisting of 25 judges each, you should expect to find very few differences between each group's averages for factors such as age, length of service, sentencing habits, or even physical height. This is because randomization serves to cancel out extreme characteristics. For every 6'7" conservative judge who is randomly assigned to a particular group, odds are that a 5'7" liberal judge will be assigned to that group as well.

Random assignment can be carried out in a variety of ways, some of which are more complex than others. Names can be drawn from a hat or a coin can be tossed. Often, however, some variant of the random number table is used. Software programs are available that use computerized methods for making group assignments, utilizing an internal random number table.

THE CONTROL GROUP

A group of subjects created through random assignment that is left in its natural state for purposes of making statistical comparisons with other experimental subject groups is called a **control group**. There are two primary reasons why every experiment should include a control group:

1. Control groups allow the researcher to assess the degree of change that has occurred in other groups as a result of a treatment or experimental condition that has been introduced.

   Because . . .

   The properly constructed control group will be identical in all respects to other groups included in an experiment, except that its subjects will not be exposed to certain changes or **treatments** that have been imposed on other groups by the researcher. It is the principle of random assignment that allows us to conclude with a high degree of confidence that all groups created at the outset of an experiment are equivalent. Therefore, it makes no difference which group of subjects created through random assignment is selected to serve as the control group. In fact, to ensure that bias has not been introduced at any level of an experiment, the group selected to serve as a control should also be selected at random.

2. Control groups permit researchers to rule out the possibility that findings of a given experiment are the result of **extraneous variables**.

   Because . . .

   The goal of a well-designed experiment is to isolate and measure the effects of a specific variable or variables, while excluding the effects of all other factors. These other factors, as you may recall from earlier discussions on causation, are extraneous variables. If an experiment lacks a proper control group, the effects of extraneous variables are allowed to creep into the research design. When this occurs, there is no way of telling whether experimental findings are due to variables of interest (introduced by the researcher) or to variables beyond the researcher's control.

THE EXPERIMENTAL GROUP

Any group composed of randomly assigned subjects that has been exposed to structured changes (i.e., treatments) imposed by the researcher(s) is referred to as an **experimental group.** Experiments can contain one or more experimental groups, each receiving a separate treatment. The findings of an experiment are determined by comparing changes in subjects belonging to experimental groups against changes in those belonging to the control group.

THE TREATMENT

Whenever researchers manipulate or change the existing conditions within a group of randomly assigned subjects they have imposed a **treatment.** In essence, it is the introduction of the treatment that defines whether subjects belong to either a control or an experimental group. You may have an image in your mind of the treatment as a pill or some type of drug that is given to one set of subjects and not the other. However, in the field of criminal justice the treatment can take on many forms. Being arrested or not being arrested can be an experimental treatment. Other examples may include the number of officers assigned to a patrol unit, whether or not prison inmates are allowed work furloughs, or even the dollar amount of a crime suspect's bail.

THE BASIC EXPERIMENT

Without adding to or taking away from the components discussed already, it is possible to construct the simplest of experimental designs. We refer to this as *the basic experiment.*

Although this design lacks complexity and is relatively easy to construct, it remains one of the most frequently used methods of modern experimentation. Simply put, the basic experiment is a highly effective research tool that produces solid, reliable findings.

In the following section, we will examine not only how to perform the basic experiment but also how this design is readily applied to situations routinely encountered by the criminal justice researcher. Bear in mind that this design is the foundation for all experiments, no matter how complex they may be. Once you have mastered the basic experiment, learning more complex experimental designs will be quite easy.

PUTTING THE PIECES TOGETHER

Let's begin with an example. Suppose you are a famous criminologist who has been working for the last 20 years (you began your career at quite an early age) on an anticrime pill. A large pharmaceutical firm would like to offer you a multi-million-dollar deal to produce this pill. However, there is one catch: The effectiveness of the anticrime pill must be demonstrated scientifically. To do so, you need do nothing more than construct a basic experiment. There are five steps involved in this process.

1. Selection of experimental subjects. First, you must make some decisions regarding the **number** of subjects required for your experiment. It is important to remember two things:

- Experimental and control groups must have the same number of subjects.
- Experimental and control groups must have a sufficient number of subjects.

Remember, the randomization process is based on the statistical probability that any initial differences between groups will tend to cancel or randomize each other out. In other words, two groups formed by random assignment will be statistically equal in all respects (that is, they will be clones of one another).

It should be noted that randomization works much better for large groups than for small groups. If we have a small number of subjects in each group, it is less likely that their differences will cancel out. Although there is no magic number to guide the selection of subjects, as a general rule experiments containing fewer than 50 subjects (25 in each group) will produce findings that are highly suspect. For random assignment, as for sample selection in general, the larger the sample, the more trustworthy the findings.

2. Random assignment of subjects. Second, the pool of subjects must be **randomly assigned** to experimental and control groups. This may be done in a variety of ways, such as drawing names from a hat, using a random number table, or even flipping a coin. The random assignment procedure need not be complicated as long as every subject has an equal probability of being placed in either the control or the experimental group. After two groups of equal size have been formed by random assignment, it is best to declare one group experimental and the other control by again using some sort of random method (e.g., a coin toss).

3. The pretesting of subjects. After experimental and control subjects have been randomly assigned to their respective groups, the next step involves conducting a **pretest**. The pretest is used to establish a statistical baseline that consists of preliminary measure(s) of the dependent variable prior to the administration of the treatment to the experimental group. It is essential that the pretest be conducted in the same manner and at the same time for all subjects. Therefore, it is always advisable to pretest subjects together, in one sitting, before they are randomly assigned to separate groups. In the hypothetical case of the anticrime pill experiments, the pretest may consist of a self-report questionnaire asking subjects a range of questions relating to their preexperimental criminal conduct.

It should be noted, however, that the pretesting of subjects is really more of a researcher's ritual than a research requirement. In fact, if random assignment is carried out correctly with a sufficient number of subjects, the pretest produces redundant information. This is true because we would expect the randomization process to balance out existing differences between the experimental and control groups. This being the case, the pretest would only confirm what we have already assumed to be true: The control and experimental groups are equal in all respects prior to carrying out the experiment.

An unnecessary pretest can actually be damaging to experimental findings. It can tip off subjects regarding the researcher's purposes for conducting the experiment. When this happens, it is easy for subjects to throw the research findings in either a positive or negative direction. Suppose, for example, that you were a participant in the anticrime pill study and you were given a pretest probing your past criminal habits. Then, immediately following the pretest, you were given a pill. Would you discover the point of the experiment? Could you make it look as if the pill worked when it really did not or vice versa? The point is that you should never use a pretest when it may reveal the experimental goal to subjects.

4. Administration of the treatment. How and when a treatment is administered are largely determined by the nature of the treatment as well as the researcher's experimental time frame. Remember that in any experiment, the treatment represents the **independent variable.** The trademark of a true experiment is that the researcher creates the treatment by manipulating the independent variable(s). In the hypothetical experiment at hand, we have one treatment and one independent variable: the effect of the anticrime pill.

Since this variable is **dichotomous** (i.e., it has two categories or levels), it will require two groups to test. The first group is the control group or the no-pill condition, and the second is the experimental group that takes the pill. Remember that the number of groups required to conduct an experiment equals the number of treatment levels (including the control level). For this reason, it is always best to reduce your treatment to the lowest possible number of levels.

There are two concepts related to the treatment phase of an experiment that you should be familiar with: one a problem and the other its cure.

- *The Hawthorne Effect (the Problem):* This effect refers to the tendency of subjects to act differently while under study than they would if they were not being studied. Any change in behavior that can be attributed to the subject's knowledge that he or she is being observed for research purposes falls under the rubric of **the Hawthorne effect.**

- *The Placebo (the Cure):* **Placebos** are artificial treatments administered to a control group. Their purpose is to simulate within the control group the actual treatment administration methods employed in the experimental group. By using placebos to ensure that control and experimental subjects are treated in an identical manner, with the exception of the actual treatment given to the experimental group, potential Hawthorne effects are neutralized or balanced out.

As you have perhaps discovered, the Hawthorne effect and the placebo go hand in hand. While the former presents a potential problem to the experimental design, the latter offers a potential cure for the problem. In our example of the anticrime pill experiment, we might encounter a Hawthorne effect in that our experimental subjects may reduce their criminal tendencies simply by virtue of taking the pill and the attention they receive from researchers while doing so.

To effectively counter these effects, we could administer a placebo to the control group in the form of a sugar pill, treating our control subjects exactly the same as we did our experimental subjects. With the introduction of the placebo, we could be confident that any bias introduced into the experimental group by virtue of the treatment procedures would exist equally in the control group. Therefore, any differences that we discover between the control and experimental groups are attributed exclusively to the treatment (i.e., the anticrime pill).

5. The posttesting of subjects. The basic experiment is completed by taking a final measurement of the dependent variable(s) in both the experimental and control groups. This is referred to as a **posttest**, regardless of whether or not a pretest was administered. Posttesting can be carried out at any one time, or on several occasions, after the treatment has been administered. Determining when is the best time to posttest depends on several factors, all of which are related to the life span of the treatment.

If you suspect that the treatment will affect subjects rapidly, then the posttest should be given quickly to capture these effects during or before the time they peak. On the other hand, if the treatment is assumed to have a slow onset and a long-term effect, you might consider conducting one or several posttests several weeks, months, or even years after the treatment was administered.

The final results of the experiment are determined by a) comparing pre- and posttest measures between experimental and control groups, or b) simply comparing posttest measures between experimental and control groups (when pretest measures are not available). Again, because of assumptions related to random assignment, both of the above methods should yield the same experimental results.

BLINDED EXPERIMENTS

The term *blinded experiment* means that either the researcher or the subjects or both do not have knowledge of who is in the experimental or control groups. If an experiment is single-blinded, this means that only the research subjects do not know whether they have been assigned to an experimental or control group. In a double-blinded experiment, both the research staff and the subjects do not know who has been assigned to the control and experimental groups. Blinding helps to keep bias, either intentional or unintentional, out of the experiment. If the researcher or the subjects don't know who is being manipulated, then it is more likely that all participants in the experiment will be treated in the same way.

EXERCISES

MULTIPLE CHOICE TEST: EXPERIMENTS

Read each statement carefully, then choose the word or phrase that correctly completes the statement.

1. The procedure that is used in an experiment to ensure that experimental and control groups are equal in all respects is
   a. random selection
   b. random assignment
   c. random allocation
   d. special selection   _____

2. A treatment given to an experimental group is the
   a. dependent variable
   b. isolation variable
   c. independent variable
   d. control effect   _____

3. The independent variable in an experiment is
   a. measured
   b. controlled
   c. manipulated
   d. isolated   _____

4. The dependent variable in an experiment is
   a. measured
   b. controlled
   c. manipulated
   d. isolated   _____

5. In order to rule out the possibility of Hawthorne effects, the researcher should administer
   a. treatments
   b. posttests
   c. pretests
   d. placebos   _____

6. The procedure used to establish a baseline measure of the dependent variable prior to conducting an experiment is called a
   a. posttest
   b. before-test
   c. pretest
   d. split-test   _____

7. When both the researchers and the subjects involved in an experiment do not have knowledge of who is in the experimental and control groups, this is called
   a. double-blinded
   b. anonymous
   c. single-blinded
   d. confidential   _____

8. The outcome of an experiment is determined by administering a posttest to the
   a. independent variable
   b. dependent variable
   c. control variable
   d. isolation variable   _____

9. As far as determining a cause and effect relationship, the experimental design is the most
   a. easy to use
   b. costly
   c. powerful
   d. inexpensive   _____

10. In the field of criminal justice, research findings determined by experiments are
   a. rare
   b. frequently found
   c. not reliable
   d. not valid   _____

IDENTIFICATION MATCH: EXPERIMENTS

Each of the following statements describes an element of the experiment. Using the key provided, match each statement with the correct element.

Key:
RA = random assignment
PT = pretest
PO = posttest
EX = experimental group
CO = control group

_____ 1. The group that is administered a placebo

_____ 2. A procedure that ensures that every subject has an equal probability of being placed in either the control group or the experimental group

_____ 3. The group that is administered the treatment

_____ 4 A test that is unnecessary if random assignment is done correctly

_____ 5. The group that could be influenced by the Hawthorne effect

_____ 6. The group that is manipulated by the researcher

_____ 7. A procedure that is often difficult to perform when conducting a criminal justice experiment

_____ 8. A test measuring the dependent variable after the treatment has been administered

_____ 9. The only true test needed to determine the outcome of an experiment

_____ 10. A test that can bias the outcome of an experiment

IS IT AN EXPERIMENT OR NOT?

The following statements describe procedures used to conduct criminal justice research. Identify whether the experimental procedures described have been carried out correctly or incorrectly.

1. Researcher X locates 45 subjects willing to participate in her experiment. She randomly assigns them to experimental and control groups.

   a. correct   **b.** incorrect

2. Researcher Y is conducting an experiment to determine the effectiveness of a new training program. However, the program is not very popular among the officer subjects participating in the experiment. To prevent potential bias in responses from the officer subjects, Researcher Y does not give a pretest prior to starting the experiment.

   a. correct   **b.** incorrect

3. Researcher X decides to double-blind his experiment, so he gives a list of the experimental and control subjects to his research assistants and instructs them not to reveal this information to the subjects.

   a. correct   **b.** incorrect

4. Researcher Y tests a new anti-gang program that involves blocking off streets to make it more difficult for gangs to engage in drive-by shootings. For 12 hours, construction workers with heavy machinery installed concrete barriers at the ends of streets in the experimental zone. Nothing was done to the streets in the control zone.

   a. correct   **b.** incorrect

5. Researcher X developed a new device to improve inmate safety in jails. She tested the device by using it on 50 newly incarcerated inmates. She gave a pretest to the inmate subjects and discovered that an average of 1 out of 5 inmates was injured in a one-month period. A posttest given to the inmates after using the device for one month revealed that not one inmate was injured. Based on these findings, Research X claims her device to be a success.

   a. correct   **b.** incorrect

MATCHING TEST: EXPERIMENTS

Insert the correct term or phrase after each definition.

random assignment   double-blinded
control group   pretest
experimental group   Hawthorne effect
single-blinded   treatment
placebo   posttest

1. The manipulation given to an experimental group

_____

2. Used to create experimental and control groups

_____

3. Used to test the dependent variable before treatment

_____

4. A test used to determine the impact of the treatment

_____

5. A group not receiving a treatment

_____

6. A group receiving a treatment

_____

7. Not revealing experimental information to subjects

_____

8. Keeping experimental information secret from everyone

_____

9. Subjects act different because they are under study

_____

10. Used to guard against Hawthorne effects

_____

SHORT ANSWER TEST: EXPERIMENTS

Answer each of the following questions in the space provided.

1. Why is the experimental design the best for determining cause and effect relationships?

_____

_____

_____

_____

_____

_____

2. Why is it so rare to find experiments in the criminal justice literature? What impact does this limitation have on the information presented in most criminal justice studies?

_____

_____

_____

_____

_____

_____

3. Why is random assignment so important in an experimental design?

_____

_____

_____

_____

_____

4. What is the importance of the placebo in experimental designs?

_____

_____

_____

_____

_____

5. Go to the Research Abstracts (located in the back of the book) and identify which of the abstracts are examples of experiments. In the space provided below, list the titles of the abstracts you chose and state briefly why you think each one is an experiment.

_____

_____

_____

_____

_____

_____

_____

_____

_____

_____

_____

_____

_____

_____

_____

_____

_____

_____

_____

_____

NAME

7

Quasi-Experiments and Time Series

LEARNING OBJECTIVE

To identify similarities and differences between the basic experiment and the quasi-experiment, using time series analysis as an example. To learn the limitations and strengths of using quasi-experimental designs to evaluate criminal justice policy.

KEY LEARNING POINTS

WHAT IS A QUASI-EXPERIMENT?

The word quasi means *as if* or *almost*. Therefore, a quasi-experiment is, literally, almost a true experiment. This is true because quasi-experiments do not contain a true control group. Rather, they contain a comparison group that is created by the researcher to act as a control group. This group cannot be called a true control group because it has not been created by random assignment. There are many varieties of quasi-experimental designs. A full discussion of these is beyond the scope of this text. In this module, we will discuss in detail the most popular type of quasi-experimental design used by criminal justice researchers: time series analysis.

TIME SERIES ANALYSIS AND TRUE EXPERIMENTS

Time series analysis is perhaps the most popular type of quasi-experimental design used in criminal justice research. This type of design is always longitudinal and involves looking at trends and cycles in specific dependent variables over time. Time series studies are either **interrupted** or **noninterrupted**. Noninterrupted time series studies simply examine changes in the dependent variable over time. For example, you might use this technique to study increases in crime rates over the last several months, years, or decades. Interrupted time series, on the other hand, include a before and after analysis. That is, the researcher is interested in examining the changes in the dependent variable not only over time, but specifically before and after some type of change has occurred. In criminal justice research, this change usually takes the form of a new law or crime prevention program. Time series are used primarily for **policy analysis.** This refers to assessing the outcomes, successes, and failures of laws and criminal justice programs.

It is possible to draw an analogy between time series designs and true experiments. Let's look at the similarities and differences between these two designs:

The subjects or objects of research. Subjects or objects of research in time series designs can be anything that shows variation over time. They can be people, cars, crime statistics, neighborhood blocks . . . anything. The key difference between time series and true experiments with respect to subjects or objects of research is the time period over which they are studied. While true experiments can be done quickly (when done in a cross-sectional time frame), subjects or objects in time series must be observed for an extended period of time. Although the time unit used could be seconds, minutes, or hours, most criminal justice research requires that days, months, or even years be used as the quasi-experimental time unit. This is so because we usually study crime-related events. Fortunately, crime-related events are relatively rare and do not happen frequently (especially serious events, like murder). So we need to perform studies that take in long time periods to capture a sufficient number of crime-related events to allow time series designs to generate stable, reliable findings.

Random assignment.   One of the key differences between time series and true experiments is in the area of random assignment. Recall that random assignment is the method by which researchers conducting true experiments create statistically equal groups (known as control and experimental groups). Without random assignment, we cannot assume that a particular treatment effect is the true cause of changes observed between experimental and control groups (i.e., pre-existing differences between groups or some outside influence other than the treatment could be producing the observed differences). Because time series designs do not use random assignment, they do not have true experimental and control groups.

Experimental and control groups.   If the time series design does not have true experimental and control groups, how is it possible to determine the effects of a treatment? The answer is simple. Time series look at the same groups of people or things over time, both **before** and **after** the introduction of a treatment. The control group is created by examining how subjects or objects react during the time period preceding the treatment. This is called a **statistical baseline.**

The experimental group consists of measuring how the same subjects or objects react after they have been introduced to the treatment. Time series designs are used often in criminal justice research because they do not require random assignment. Remember, when we perform random assignment we run the risk of giving something to or taking something away from some subjects. Many potential criminal justice issues, such as death penalty laws and psychological treatments, simply do not permit the use of random assignment.

The treatment. The term most often used for treatments in quasi-experiments is **intervention.** An intervention can be created by the researcher or can occur naturally. The ability of a time series design to capture changes produced by naturally occurring events makes this design very useful to criminal justice researchers. For example, it is possible to capture changes in citizens' attitudes toward police produced by riots, changes produced in gang homicide rates by introducing tougher juvenile sentencing laws, or even changes in police officers' use of force tactics after the introduction of a new intermediate force technique.

Independent and dependent variables. In a time series design, as in a true experiment, the dependent variable is the group or object that is being measured for change. Each observation of the dependent variable over time in a time series is like one subject added to a true experiment. Therefore, the sample size of a quasi-experiment depends upon how may different points in time at which the dependent variable is measured. This is why it is important to obtain a sufficient number of data points in time when conducting a quasi-experiment.

On the other hand, the independent variable in a time series is most likely the intervention. For example, if you examined the effects of the Three Strikes Law on the number of persons who are sentenced to prison, the independent variable would be the Three Strikes Law. It would have two attributes: presence of the law (after the law was passed) and absence of the law (before the law was passed).

In the case of noninterrupted time series designs, the independent variable in a time series can be time itself. For example, you could study the effects that time has on gang membership. In this case there would be no intervention. You would simply measure gang membership over time and attribute increases or decreases in gang membership trends to time.

INTERNAL INVALIDITY ISSUES

Like an experiment, a time series is subject to internal invalidity. Just to refresh your memory, internal invalidity occurs when some outside variable other than the independent variable is causing change in the dependent variable. In other words, an internally invalid experiment is one in which we think the treatment or intervention is causing our findings, but some other influence or variable is really at work.

In time series designs, we want to discover what is called a **true trend.** A true trend is an increase or decrease in the dependent variable that is caused by the intervention. That is, when we say we have found a true trend in a time series, we are concluding that our intervention has produced a reliable change in our dependent variable over time.

There are, however, some naturally occurring events that cause time trends to suggest we have a true trend when, in fact, we don't have one. These sources of internal invalidity for quasi-experiments include seasonal effects, cyclical effects, and abnormal events.

Seasonal effects. Seasonal effects are regular fluctuations in the dependent variable that occur within a period of one year. Crime is very subject to seasonal effects. Homicide rates, for example, go up in December, down in February, and up again in July. If you were to construct a quasi-experiment on homicide rates that had its intervention at the end of July, you might think that the decrease in murders you observed was due to your treatment (perhaps a new get-tough-on-crime program). In fact, you may be observing simply a naturally occurring seasonal trend.

Cyclical effects. Cyclical effects are similar to seasonal effects, except they occur over a period of years in time. Crime rates are also cyclical. If you examine the *UCR* it is easy to see how crime in the U.S. has cycled over past decades. From the late 60s until 1980, crime was on the increase. During the 1980s crime appeared to level off. In the 1990s crime has been decreasing. Again, you must remember that cycling of crime can be misleading.

Abnormal events. An abnormal event is anything that happens during or around the time you introduce your intervention. It may have the same effect on the dependent variable as your intervention. Suppose you are studying the effects of a new antidrug educational program in elementary schools, similar to DARE. At the time you started the new DARE program, police were conducting a series of undercover narcotics arrests in schools. Could it be that the decrease in the use of and interest in drugs you discovered in your quasi-experimental study was due to the police activity, and not due to your intervention (i.e., the new DARE program)? This is an example of an abnormal event effect, rather than a true trend.

HOW TO PROTECT AGAINST INTERNAL INVALIDITY

The best way to protect your time series study from internal invalidity is to use as many data points as you can both before and after your intervention. If you measure your dependent variable for a long enough period of time both preceding and following your intervention, you can easily spot seasonal effects. Cyclical effects over an extended period of years are much more difficult to detect. Abnormal events usually do not last for a long period of time, so they too should be easy to separate from true trends.

NONEQUIVALENT GROUPS AND MATCHING

Another type of quasi-experimental design involves the creation of **nonequivalent groups** or **matching**. In this technique, researchers create a control group by simply finding some other group that is very similar to the group that is being studied (or given a treatment or intervention) and using this group in their comparisons. For example, a researcher who is studying the impact of a new crime prevention program in a specific neighborhood may choose another neighborhood that is very similar with respect to size and demographics to compare to the experimental neighborhood. This technique can also be used to strengthen the findings from a time series design. For example, you can match several nonequivalent groups to a particular group that you are studying over time. Differences over time between the group you are examining and the matched groups will further strengthen the validity of your findings from a time series design.

EXERCISES

MULTIPLE CHOICE TEST: QUASI-EXPERIMENTS

Read each statement carefully, then choose the word or phrase that correctly completes the statement.

1. The type of analysis involving evaluation of programs and changes in the criminal justice system for which quasi-experiments are especially well suited is called
    a. special evaluation
    b. policy analysis
    c. program trending
    d. policy specification   _____

2. A special type of quasi-experiment involving a longitudinal examination of the dependent variable is called
    a. nonequivalent groups
    b. patterning
    c. trending
    d. time series   _____

3. Quasi-experiments based on nonequivalent groups involve
    a. random assignment
    b. true control groups
    c. matched groups
    d. unmatched groups   _____

4. In a time series study, the intervention is a (an)
    a. independent variable
    b. dependent variable
    c. control group
    d. experimental group   _____

5. In a typical before and after design, the period before the intervention acts as a (an)
    a. independent variable
    b. dependent variable

    c. control group

    d. quasi-experimental group   _____

6. A time series design that does not have an intervention is called

    a. interrupted

    b. nonequivalent

    c. equivalent

    d. noninterrupted   _____

7. Cyclical and seasonal effects are sources of

    a. true trends

    b. reliability

    c. validity

    d. internal invalidity   _____

8. Compared to experiments, quasi-experiments are

    a. more powerful

    b. as powerful

    c. less powerful

    d. more efficient   _____

9. Which of the following are not sources of internal invalidity in a time series study?

    a. cyclical effects

    b. seasonal effects

    c. true trends

    d. abnormal events   _____

10. Which of the following quasi-experiments would not be used to evaluate the impact of a program change in the criminal justice system?

    a. nonequivalent groups

    b. noninterrupted time series

    c. interrupted time series

    d. both a and b   _____

IDENTIFICATION MATCH: QUASI-EXPERIMENTS

Each of the following statements describes a situation in which either a noninterrupted time series or an interrupted time series should be used. Using the key provided, match each statement with the appropriate time series design.

Key:
IN = interrupted time series
NO = noninterrupted time series

_____ 1. An evaluation of a new drunk driving law

_____ 2. Citizen attitudes toward the death penalty from 1950 to 1998

_____ 3. Changes in police arrest rates since the Rodney King incident

_____ 4. Changes in the *Uniform Crime Reports* since 1940

_____ 5. The impact of the three strikes law on the U.S. crime rate

_____ 6. A program analysis of community policing

_____ 7. A longitudinal study of victimization trends

_____ 8. Public support for the F.B.I. after the Waco and Ruby Ridge incidents

_____ 9. A comparison of drug use in urban and rural high schools over time

_____ 10. The impact of the TV show, *America's Most Wanted,* on arrest rates

EXPERIMENT AND QUASI-EXPERIMENT ANALOGY

In the exercise below, identify which of the components of a quasi-experiment are equivalent (i.e., as if or almost the same) to those of a true experiment.

1. The intervention in a quasi-experiment is equivalent to the _____ in an experiment.
   a. independent variable
   b. dependent variable
   c. control group
   d. experimental group

2. The before condition in a time series is equivalent to the _____ in an experiment.
   a. independent variable
   b. dependent variable
   c. control group
   d. experimental group

3. The matched group in a nonequivalent quasi-experiment is equivalent to the _____ in an experiment.
   a. independent variable
   b. dependent variable
   c. control group
   d. experimental group

4. The after condition in a time series is equivalent to the _____ in an experiment.
   a. independent variable
   b. dependent variable
   c. control group
   d. experimental group

5. The units of time in a time series design are equivalent to the _____ in an experiment.
   a. treatment
   b. subjects
   c. placebo
   d. random assignment

MATCHING TEST: QUASI-EXPERIMENTS

Insert the correct term or phrase after each definition.

policy analysis   noninterrupted
time series   seasonal effect
matched groups   cyclical effect
intervention   abnormal event
true trend   interrupted

1. An independent variable in interrupted time series

2. A short-term source of internal invalidity

3. A trend showing the impact of an intervention

4. Type of time series used for policy analysis

5. A long-term source of internal invalidity

6. A source of internal invalidity that occurs at the same time as the intervention

7. A type of evaluation method using quasi-experiments

8. A quasi-experiment involving a researcher-created control group

9. A quasi-experiment that is always longitudinal in nature

10. A type of time series not including an intervention

SHORT ANSWER TEST: QUASI-EXPERIMENTS

Answer each of the following questions in the space provided.

1. Why are quasi-experiments more likely to be used in criminal justice research than are true experiments?

_____

_____

_____

_____

_____

_____

_____

_____

_____

2. What are the potential hazards of conducting an interrupted time series study by measuring the dependent variable at only one time before the intervention and only one time after the intervention?

_____

_____

_____

_____

_____

_____

_____

_____

_____

3. Give two examples of current issues or topics related to the criminal justice system (e.g., from television, magazines, or newspapers) that could be studied by quasi-experiments, and briefly explain how.

_____

_____

_____

_____

_____

_____

_____

_____

_____

_____

_____

_____

_____

4. Go to the Research Abstracts (located in the back of the book) and identify which of the abstracts are examples of quasi-experiments. In the spaces provided below, list the titles of the abstracts you chose and state briefly why you think they are quasi-experiments.

_____

_____

_____

_____

_____

_____

NAME

The Criminal Justice Nonexperiment

LEARNING OBJECTIVE

To be able to distinguish between the nonexperimental design and other research designs (e.g., true and quasi-experimental). To understand the various limitations of research findings generated by nonexperimental designs. To discover the value of nonexperimental designs for performing descriptive research and to recognize the hazards of using such designs for drawing causal conclusions.

KEY LEARNING POINTS

WHAT ARE NONEXPERIMENTAL DESIGNS?

Nonexperimental designs are typically carried out in the form of surveys or interviews. This type of research has subjects (known as **respondents**), but in no way manipulates or controls the subjects. Therefore, the nonexperimental design has no means of establishing a control group. Without a control group, findings based on nonexperimental designs are extremely open to internal invalidity problems.

This is why the nonexperimental design seldom allows us to draw causal conclusions from its findings.

THE VALUE OF NONEXPERIMENTAL DESIGNS: DESCRIPTION

Nonexperimental designs are not totally useless. To the contrary, they are very good for conducting cross-sectional studies for purposes of describing subjects, groups, or objects of research. In many respects, this type of design provides a snapshot or profile of the way things are during a certain specific time period. Quite frankly, the majority of criminal justice research that deals with people's attitudes or opinions about police, courts, or corrections topics is done using nonexperimental designs.

THE HAZARDS OF NONEXPERIMENTAL DESIGNS: CAUSATION

When we want to find out the cause of something, we would prefer to use a true experiment (first) or a quasi-experiment (second). There are many reasons why nonexperimental designs should be our last choice when we want to find out the true causes of a problem. Remember, the biggest enemy to research designs is internal invalidity.

When internal invalidity exists, the effects of variables other than the independent variable creep into the design and possibly affect the dependent variable. When these extraneous effects do in fact creep in, we are never sure whether our findings are the result of the independent variable or the result of other variables that crept into the research design.

Always remember this: Control groups keep extraneous effects out of research designs and allow us to assume that the independent variable is causing the dependent variable to change. Unfortunately, the nonexperimental design has no control group; therefore, there is a fair to good chance that our research findings from these designs have been contaminated by the effects of outside variables (or extraneous effects). If a group tries to claim they have found the cause of something, but they are using a nonexperimental design, be cautious about believing the findings.

SPURIOUS EFFECTS AND INTERVENING VARIABLE EFFECTS

There are many sources of contamination that can render a nonexperimental design's results invalid. However, there are two situations that tend to be very common. The first is called a **spurious effect** or sometimes a **third variable effect**. The second is called an **intervening variable effect**. The following examples demonstrate how important it is to be on guard for these.

EXAMPLE ONE: CRIME AND THE MOON

Everyone has heard of the old tale that when the moon is full, people are more likely to act crazy. Many police officers say that there is more crime on nights when there is a full moon. Is this true? Well, there is some research that indicates this old tale is indeed true. But why?

Let's consider the brain wave theory. One researcher assumed that when the moon is full, its pull places more gravitational pressure on the brain. This pressure, in turn, causes some people to go wild and lose control. Under this theory, we assume that the moon is directly causing deviant or criminal behavior. In fact, the researcher conducted a survey of 2,000 criminals and discovered that a majority of them committed their crimes during full moons. Does this finding support the brain wave theory?

Well, it could—but it probably is the result of a spurious variable effect. Figure 8-1 shows how a spurious variable effect makes it look as if an independent variable, the full moon (A), is causing the dependent variable, crime (B). But something else is really going on. It is actually what the independent and dependent variables share in common with the spurious variable, light (C), that is making the researcher think that the moon is causing crime.

EXAMPLE TWO: INTERVENING VARIABLE EFFECTS

Another typical situation that causes nonexperimental designs to produce false conclusions is the intervening variable effect. In this case, the independent variable and the dependent variable are held together by a third variable in

FIGURE 8-1

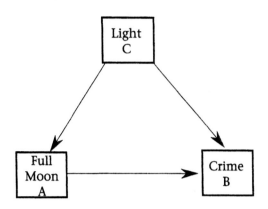

between them. This variable in between (i.e., the intervening variable) acts almost like glue sticking the independent variable and the dependent variable together, when in fact the independent and dependent variables really have nothing in common. Figure 8-2 depicts an intervening variable effect.

Consider the case of research done to determine why a person becomes the victim of a crime, or the study of victimization. When the study of victimization was first being established in the mid-1970s, researchers discovered that the probability of becoming a crime victim was significantly higher for young males (in their late teens to early twenties) who were unmarried. If you were to draw a causal conclusion from this information, which many researchers did, you would assume that being a young, unmarried male would cause a person to become a crime victim.

On the other hand, a group of researchers called routine activities theorists claimed that the direct effects model of victimization was wrong, the product of an intervening variable effect. They assumed that there was in fact a hidden variable between being a young, unmarried male (the IV) and becoming a crime victim (the DV). This hidden variable was a person's routine pattern of activities.

FIGURE 8-2

A ⟶ C ⟶ B   A ⟵ C ⟶ B

To make a long story short, there is now considerable evidence to suggest that the routine activities theorists were right. The proper causal relationship for victimization should look something like Figure 8-3 (where "routine activities" is the intervening variable).

PATH MODELS AND DIAGRAMMING

Because nonexperimental designs often contain many relationships between many variables, it is helpful to create a map of these relationships called a **path model** or **path diagram**. The illustration in Figure 8-3 is an example of a path model. The components of a path model have their own distinct language. Specifically, the relationships in the model are either **direct effects** or **indirect effects**. The variables included in the model are either **endogenous** or **exogenous**. Direct effects are simply relationships between two variables in the model that do not have another variable coming between them (e.g., the path between Gender and R.A. [Routine Activities]). A relationship between two variables that has one or more variables intervening between them is an indirect effect (e.g., the path between Gender, R.A., and Crime). Exogenous variables are the independent variable effects in the model (e.g., Gender and Age on R.A. and R.A. on Crime). Endogenous variables are the dependent variable effects in the model (e.g., R.A. and Crime).

FIGURE 8-3

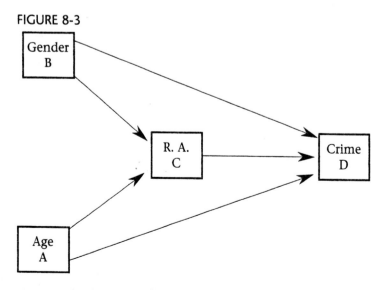

WHAT ABOUT STATISTICAL CONTROLS?

Nonexperimental designs do provide some means for controls, or making things equal between groups or objects of research. However, these controls are imposed through statistical means and they in no way guarantee that all external sources of internal validity will be kept out of the design. Making things statistically equal in a nonexperimental design requires a large number of subjects.

For example, we may want to conduct a survey comparing the differences in job satisfaction between police officers who work footbeats and those who work patrol car assignments. We could just compare footbeat and patrol officers' opinions, but could we say that any differences between them are only due to differences in the type of assignment they work? Of course not. There may be many other spurious or intervening effects causing these differences. To rule out differences that are not produced by the independent variable, we could make things statistically equal between the two groups (that is, we create two statistically equal groups, similar to the ones that would be created by random assignment).

To do this, we must match footbeat and patrol officers on many different background characteristics, such as age, training, length of time on the force, race, gender, shift, and so forth. Only then could we assume that there is a difference between footbeat and patrol officers due to their type of assignment, with everything else being equal. It is "everything else" that is very difficult to control for statistically within the nonexperimental model.

EXERCISES

MULTIPLE CHOICE TEST: NONEXPERIMENTS

Read each statement carefully, then choose the word or phrase that correctly completes the statement.

1. Variable relationships in nonexperimental designs are
   a. cause and effect
   b. correlational
   c. powerful
   d. both a and c   _____

2. The method used to map out possible variable relationships in a nonexperimental design is called a
   a. flow chart
   b. decision tree
   c. path model
   d. variable map   _____

3. A relationship between variables that appears to be strong, but is really the product of what the variables have in common with a third variable, is called
   a. causal
   b. spurious
   c. experimental
   d. intervening   _____

4. Intervening variable relationships in a nonexperimental design are a source of
   a. internal invalidity
   b. validity
   c. reliability
   d. power   _____

5. Checking for possible sources of internal invalidity in nonexperimental designs is done by using
   a. true control groups
   b. statistical controls

    c. quasi control groups

    d. matching   _____

6. The least powerful, and most common, design for conducting criminal justice research is

    a. experimental

    b. nonexperimental

    c. quasi-experimental

    d. time series   _____

7. Relationships between variables that are linked in a path model without another variable coming between them are

    a. direct

    b. indirect

    c. inter-causal

    d. third-order   _____

8. Relationships between variables that are linked in a path model with one or more variables coming between them are

    a. direct

    b. indirect

    c. inter-causal

    d. third-order   _____

9. A variable that precedes another in a path model is

    a. exogenous

    b. endogenous

    c. dependent

    d. indirect   _____

10. A variable that follows another in a path model is

    a. exogenous

    b. endogenous

    c. independent

    d. indirect   _____

IDENTIFICATION MATCH: NONEXPERIMENTS

Each of the following statements describes an element of a path model. Using the key provided, match each statement with the correct path model element.

Key:
IR = indirect relationship
DR = direct relationship
EX = exogenous variable
EN = endogenous variable

_____ 1. In the relationship A→B, what is variable A?

_____ 2. In the relationship A→B, what is variable B?

_____ 3. In the relationship A→B→C, what is variable A to variable C?

_____ 4. In the relationship A→B→C, what is variable B to variable C?

_____ 5. The relationship X→Y→Z is what?

_____ 6. The relationship X→Y is?

_____ 7. In the relationship A→B→C→D, what is the relationship between A and D?

_____ 8. In the relationship A→B→C→D, what is the relationship between A and B?

_____ 9. In the relationship A→B→C→D, what is variable C to variable B?

_____ 10. In the relationship A←C→B, what is variable C to variable A?

MATCHING TEST: NONEXPERIMENTS

Insert the correct term or phrase after each definition.

nonexperiment   direct effect
correlated   indirect effect
spurious   statistical controls
intervening   path model
exogenous   endogenous

1. A variable that comes between two variables

_____

2. A method used to chart nonexperimental relationships

_____

3. The equivalent to an independent variable in a path model

_____

4. The equivalent to a dependent variable in a path model

_____

5. A research design that does not have a control group

_____

6. A variable effect caused by an intervening variable

_____

7. A term used to describe variables that move together

_____

8. Used in place of a control group in nonexperiments

_____

9. Otherwise known as a third variable relationship

_____

10. A relationship between one exogenous and one endogenous variable

_____

SHORT ANSWER TEST: NONEXPERIMENTS

Answer each of the following questions in the space provided.

1. Considering the moon and crime example in this module, how would you create a test to remove spurious variable effects to show that it is light, and not a full moon, that is causing crime?

_____

2. Considering the victimization example (routine activities theory) in this module, how would you create a test to remove the intervening variable effect to show that it is routine activities and not demographic background that is causing victimization?

_____

3. Draw a figure representing a spurious variable effect and an intervening variable effect that concerns a variable relationship related to a criminal justice issue. Explain this relationship and why it is an example of a spurious variable effect.

_____

_____

_____

_____

_____

_____

_____

_____

_____

_____

_____

_____

_____

_____

_____

_____

4. Go to the Research Abstracts (located in the back of the book) and identify which of the abstracts are examples of nonexperiments. In the space provided below, list the titles of the abstracts you chose and state briefly why you think they are nonexperiments.

_____

_____

_____

_____

_____

_____

_____

_____

_____

_____

_____

NAME

9

Surveys, Part I: Asking Questions about Criminal Justice Issues

LEARNING OBJECTIVE

To learn the proper techniques for creating properly worded questions for surveys or questionnaires.

KEY LEARNING POINTS

SURVEY QUESTIONS MUST RELATE TO YOUR HYPOTHESES

Remember, hypotheses are if-then questions about your theory. Your survey questions are going to provide you with answers to your hypotheses. **Each survey question should relate specifically to either an independent variable or a dependent variable in one your hypotheses.** For example:

YOUR THEORY
Domestic violence is a product of alcohol abuse.

YOUR HYPOTHESIS
If a spouse is an alcoholic
then he or she is likely to be an abusive spouse.

How much alcohol do you drink in a typical week?
[ ] none or 1 drink [ ] 2 drinks [ ] 3 or more drinks

In the above example, you can see clearly that the theory, hypothesis, and survey questions are related. The theory advances a general idea about what causes domestic violence (i.e., alcohol abuse); the hypothesis, which is directional, assumes that persons who abuse alcohol are more likely to abuse their spouses. Finally, the survey question is designed to obtain a measure of how much a person drinks. This hypothesis addresses the independent variable in the hypothesis. Another survey question can be written to measure the dependent variable in the hypothesis, which is spousal abuse.

HOW TO WORD SURVEY QUESTIONS

How you word your questions will ultimately determine the quality of your survey data. Changing even one word in a survey question can cause a person to answer in a totally different way. The rule to remember is that there is not one right way to word a survey question, but there are several wrong ways. Here are some of the important things that you **should not** do when wording your survey questions:

1. Don't use vague or technical language in your survey questions. What appears as **vague** or technical language to you may or may not be vague or technical to someone else, namely the person you plan to have answer the survey. In the field of criminal justice, we use many words that are not used in everyday language. Even words such as jail and prison are easily confused (although you no doubt know the difference from your corrections class). Police officer and sheriff mean different things to us in the field of criminal justice than they do to the general population. Many people may not know that police officers usually serve in municipal jurisdictions, or that deputy sheriffs usually operate jails, or that prisons are operated at the state level. However, the

accuracy of a survey about police functions would be affected if people answering the survey were confused over the
terms police officer and deputy sheriff.

2. Don't make your questions too long. The ideal length
for a survey question is about 20 to 25 words. A question
longer than this can cause the person answering the survey
to lose focus on the task of answering the survey and result
in less than accurate responses. Compare the following two
questions:

> Q1: Prisoners are generally dissatisfied with the sur-
> roundings of the prison in which they are housed
> because they do not like being confined to small cells
> and recreation yards that are usually poorly maintained.
> Do you agree or disagree with this statement?

> Q2: Would you agree or disagree that most prisoners do
> not like where they are being housed?

Question #2 is much easier to read than Question #1. Time is
valuable to everyone, including people who are answering
surveys. Keep your questions short in order to keep your survey respondents interested in the question. If they become
disinterested, they either will not answer at all or will give
you an answer that has been given very little thought.

3. Don't ask questions that are loaded or unbalanced.
When a question is **loaded** it leads the reader in some definite direction. That is, the question doesn't provide both
sides of the story. For example, consider the following loaded
question:

> Do you agree that laws for career criminals are getting
> tougher?

The above question is loaded because it doesn't present both
sides of the argument; that is, the position of those who disagree is missing. The balanced version of this question is:

> Do you agree or disagree that laws for career criminals
> are getting tougher?

Loaded questions generally cause a person to answer in the direction in which the question is loaded. This is particularly true when the question is also unclear.

4. Load a question when you feel it is necessary to get a truthful answer. In certain cases, you **need to load** a question. Loading is most often used to obtain answers to sensitive or embarrassing questions. Detectives often use a loading technique to elicit confessions from suspects. Although we are not in the business of asking for confessions, there are times when a criminal justice researcher must ask a question that is emotionally difficult for a person to answer. This is especially true when questions must probe for answers to things such as:

* drug use,
* prior victimization experiences,
* prior offending behavior.

For example, suppose you want to conduct a survey of maximum security prison inmates. Specifically, you want to find out how they feel regarding homosexual activity in prison. If you ask the following balanced question, you might not get truthful answers:

> Do you agree or disagree that there is homosexual activity in your prison?

Because homosexual activity in prison environments is a very sensitive issue, many inmates may disagree with the above question (i.e., state that there is no homosexual activity). However, you are well aware that homosexual activity exists in most custodial environments. So write a question that cuts to the chase and breaks the ice right away, like this:

> When was the last time you were aware of a homosexual activity in your cell block?

Inmates will be more likely to give a truthful answer to the above question because it immediately crosses the sensitivity barrier and allows for open discussion of the sensitive topic.

5. Don't construct a conjunction question. A conjunction **question** is really two questions linked by words like *and*. In other words, the questions are really two questions that have been made into one. Here is an example:

> Should Supreme Court Justices serve life terms and should they be required to hear all cases relating to the death penalty?

There are really two questions, and the respondents might want to answer "yes" to the first question and "no" to the second question (or vice versa). To word this question correctly, split it into two separate questions.

6. Don't use a false premise. False premise questions are so absurd, ridiculous, or offensive that a person has a difficult time answering them. These questions are usually phrased as hypotheticals or what-ifs. For example:

> How much money would I have to pay you to engage police in a low-speed pursuit like the one led by O.J. Simpson in Los Angeles?

Clearly, some people would think the above question is either so funny or so offensive that they could not or would not take it seriously. When this happens, you are likely to get answers that are unreliable.

7. Watch out for prestige bias. Prestige bias occurs when the name of an important place or person is included in your question. Rather than making the respondent think more about your question, an important name or place may bias a person's response. Consider the following questions:

Without Bias

Do you favor or disfavor the use of secret police to arrest dangerous offenders?

With Bias

The Nazis were the first to use secret police. Do you favor or disfavor the use of secret police to arrest dangerous offenders?

Although the two questions ask the same thing, the second one includes bias. By associating the idea of secret police with the word *Nazi*, we may have stirred some emotion or ideas in your mind that would cause you to react differently to the second question than you did to the first. The rule here is to leave out specific names, places, or other identifiers that are irrelevant to the question you are asking.

8. Avoid asking about intentions to act. When you ask a question that concerns a future action, you must ground it in the present moment. In other words, you can never ask people about their **intention to act** because nobody knows today how they will act tomorrow. When you want to find out about how someone might act at a later date, ask them how they would act or feel about the future event if it occurred right now. For example, you would ask the following question if you wanted to inquire about future voting behavior on an anticrime bill:

> If you were to vote today, would you vote for or against the state's new anticrime bill?

Don't ask, "Are you going to vote for the anticrime bill next month?" There is no guarantee that a "yes" answer today will result in action on voting day.

9. Don't speak in the double negative. A double negative occurs when the question contains two (or perhaps more) words that are negative in meaning. Consider the following double negative question:

> Do you find it not uncommon for gang members to never write graffiti on park benches?

Do you have any difficulty in answering this question? If you answer "yes," doesn't it really mean "no?" If you run into a double negative situation, it is best to reword the question in a simple balanced format:

> Do you find it common or uncommon for gang members to write graffiti on park benches?

EXERCISES

MULTIPLE CHOICE TEST: SURVEY QUESTIONS

Read each statement carefully, then choose the word or phrase that correctly completes the statement.

1. A survey question that uses words that are specific to the field of criminal justice is an example of a
   a. loaded question
   b. balanced question
   c. vague question
   d. false premise question   _____

2. A survey question that is actually made up of two separate questions is a
   a. loaded question
   b. conjunction question
   c. prestige bias question
   d. balanced question   _____

3. Including the name of an important place or person in a survey question may lead to
   a. prestige bias
   b. double negative
   c. intention to act
   d. vague questions   _____

4. The length of a survey question should be
   a. 10–20 words
   b. 20–25 words
   c. 30–40 words
   d. 40–50 words   _____

5. Survey questions that lead someone in one definite direction are
   a. loaded
   b. too technical
   c. double negative
   d. too vague   _____

6. Survey questions that are absurd, ridiculous, or offensive may lead to bias caused by
   a. prestige bias
   b. intention to act
   c. false premise
   d. double negative   _____

7. Including a statement in a survey question such as *not uncommon* may confuse readers because it is a (an)
   a. prestige bias
   b. intention to act
   c. false premise
   d. double negative   _____

8. A survey question that concerns a future action deals with
   a. prestige bias
   b. intention to act
   c. false premise
   d. double negative   _____

9. When survey questions are difficult to answer because they are either sensitive or embarrassing to the reader, the questions should be
   a. loaded
   b. lengthened
   c. shortened
   d. reworded   _____

10. Survey questions should relate to
   a. independent variables
   b. dependent variables
   c. random ideas
   d. both a and b   _____

IDENTIFICATION MATCH: SURVEY QUESTIONS

Each of the following statements describes an incorrectly worded survey question. Using the key provided, match each statement with the problem it represents.

Key:
VA = too vague or too technical
FP = false premise
CO = conjunctive question
IN = intention to act
LO = loaded question

_____ 1. Do you agree that the death penalty should be decided by a jury?

_____ 2. Should children under the age of 10 be allowed to purchase guns?

_____ 3. Are you willing to become a reserve police officer next year?

_____ 4. Are prisons safe for prisoners and correctional officers?

_____ 5. Do you believe that pat-down searches violate due process?

_____ 6. Will you vote for the District Attorney in the next election?

_____ 7. Is it a good idea for police to engage in high-speed pursuits?

_____ 8. Should boiling in oil be allowed as a punishment for speeders?

_____ 9. In your opinion, should DNA be allowed as evidence in court?

_____ 10. Are police well-liked or do they respond quickly in your neighborhood?

MATCHING TEST: SURVEY QUESTIONS

Insert the correct term or phrase after each definition.

vague language   false premise
excessive length   prestige bias
loading   intention to act
conjunction question   double negative
pretest   survey questions

1. Necessary when questions are sensitive or embarrassing

   _____

2. Must be based on variables in research hypotheses

   _____

3. Should be used to test the quality of survey questions

   _____

4. Survey question over 25 words

   _____

5. Survey question containing the words *and* and *or*

   _____

6. Survey question containing words like *not unlikely*

   _____

7. Survey question containing famous names and places

   _____

8. Survey question that is unbalanced

   _____

9. Survey question that is unbelievable

   _____

10. Asking survey respondents to forecast future behavior

    _____

SHORT ANSWER TEST: SURVEY QUESTIONS

Answer each of the following questions in the space provided.

1. Explain how question wording relates to a study's hypothesis (and in particular the independent and dependent variables).

    _____

    _____

    _____

    _____

    _____

    _____

    _____

2. How can questions that are worded improperly affect the quality of the data gathered by using a questionnaire? Be specific, using examples of specific question wording problems discussed in this module (e.g., too long, too vague).

    _____

    _____

    _____

    _____

    _____

    _____

    _____

    _____

    _____

3. Write one question that is worded correctly and one that
    is worded incorrectly for each of the nine rules discussed
    in this module.

    Vague or technical language

    _____

    _____

    _____

    _____

    _____

    _____

    Too long

    _____

    _____

    _____

    _____

    _____

    _____

    Loaded or unbalanced

    _____

    _____

    _____

    _____

    _____

    _____

    Necessary loaded question

    _____

    _____

    _____

Conjunction question

False premise

Prestige bias

Intention to act

_____

_____

_____

_____

Double negative

_____

_____

_____

_____

_____

10

Surveys, Part II: Providing Answers to Survey Questions

LEARNING OBJECTIVE

To be able to compose both open- and closed-ended answers to survey questions. To understand the various types of scaled responses to criminal justice questions and when it is appropriate to use them.

KEY LEARNING POINTS

OPEN-ENDED RESPONSES

Open-ended responses are simply answers to questions that are written in by the respondent. All that is needed for an open-ended response is for the researcher to leave a space following a question for the respondent to fill in an answer. It is advisable to use this method only when your survey is to be completed by a small group. It is very difficult to sift through large numbers of written responses and make sense out of them. Remember, you will have to provide some sort of analysis of your survey responses. If your responses are written, you will have to analyze them by grouping them based on common ideas or themes. This is a very time-consuming and difficult process. In addition, the precision of your analysis will be reduced when you (the researcher) have to make judgement calls about what is meant by someone's written response.

There is some research to support the idea that open-ended questions are best for gathering information about sensitive or embarrassing issues and experiences. The logic is that respondents feel better about expressing emotionally charged responses in their own words. Therefore, when dealing with criminal justice topics like victimization and sexual offending, the open-ended answer format may be especially useful.

CLOSED-ENDED RESPONSES

Most often, criminal justice survey research is conducted using **closed-ended** responses. This means that responses are provided by the researcher and are usually filled in, circled, or checked off by the person completing the survey. Closed-ended responses are best to use when the group that is to be surveyed is moderate to large in size. It is very easy to enter the results from closed-ended responses into a computer database for quick analysis.

Closed-ended responses can range in complexity from a simple yes or no format to very elaborate scales and indexes. Regardless of how complicated your closed-ended responses are, you must always be sure that they are **exhaustive** and **mutually exclusive**.

1. Exhaustiveness. Closed-ended responses are exhaustive when they include all possible ways a person could answer a question. For example, consider the following question for police officers and closed-ended responses to it:

Question:

What is your current rank?

Incorrect Responses:

[ ] Patrol Officer
[ ] Sergeant
[ ] Captain
[ ] Chief

Correct Responses:

[ ] Patrol Officer
[ ] Sergeant
[ ] Detective
[ ] Lieutenant
[ ] Captain
[ ] Commander
[ ] Deputy Chief
[ ] Chief
[ ] Other _____

The first question violates the rule of exhaustiveness because it does not include all police officer ranks. If all ranks are not included in the question responses, some respondents cannot correctly answer the question. This is when the word **other** becomes useful. Whenever you are unsure that your closed-ended responses are exhaustive, you can always include the category *other* to catch any unplanned responses. However, one word of caution is in order: *Use* other *only when there will be a small number of respondents.* If large numbers of responses fall into the *other* category, chances are you have omitted a significant category from your closed-ended responses.

2. Mutual Exclusiveness. When we say that closed-ended responses are mutually exclusive, we mean that they do not overlap in meaning. In other words, the response categories are clearly distinct from one another and do not confuse the person reading them. The following closed-ended responses violate the mutual exclusivity rule:

Question:

Would you prosecute a suspect for petty theft?
[ ] Definitely would prosecute
[ ] Probably would prosecute
[ ] Probably would not prosecute
[ ] Definitely would not prosecute

The problem with the above question lies in the middle two categories: "Probably would . . . would not prosecute." In actuality, there is no difference between these responses. They both say that the prosecutor might prosecute. The person responding to this question could have answered the second response or the third response because the categories overlap (i.e., they are not mutually exclusive). To make the responses mutually exclusive, the example should be worded as follows:

[ ] Definitely would prosecute

[ ] Might prosecute

[ ] Definitely would not prosecute

SCALES

Scales are response categories that measure degrees of difference in attitudes, opinions, feelings, or whatever is being measured. The most common and widely used scale in criminal justice research is known as the **Likert scale**. These scales have been around for decades and their effectiveness has been established repeatedly in numerous research studies. No doubt you have seen or used a Likert scale before, like the one used for responding to this question:

To what extent do you agree with the statement: "The FBI should be giving more extensive training to its agents in the area of antiterrorism tactics."

[ ] Strongly agree

[ ] Agree

[ ] Neither agree nor disagree

[ ] Disagree

[ ] Strongly disagree

Likert scales, like all other scales, have balanced response categories. That is, there is a neutral or center response (Neither agree nor disagree) with equivalent positive (Agree, Strongly agree) and negative (Disagree, Strongly disagree) responses on either side of it.

The responses in a Likert scale are referred to as **points.** The example has five response categories, so it has five points. The five-point Likert scale is the one most commonly used in criminal justice research. However, Likert scales can have as few as three points (e.g., Always, Sometimes, Never) or as many as seven, nine, or eleven points. Here is an example of a nine-point Likert scale:

> To what extent do you agree or disagree with the statement: "More jails should be built specifically to house hard-core gang members."

Strongly Agree   Strongly Disagree

1 2 3 4 5 6 7 8 9

In the above example, a respondent would circle the number from 1 to 9 that best expressed his or her opinion. As you may have noticed, when using Likert scales that have more than five points, specific words to describe each response category (e.g., Agree, Disagree) cannot be used. Instead, numbers ranging from the extreme positive (Strongly Agree) to the extreme negative (Strongly Disagree) are used.

HOW MANY POINTS TO USE

If you decide to use a scale in your survey, always begin with a five-point Likert scale. Then, pretest your survey instrument. If you find that 90% or more of your responses are falling into just one of the response categories (in other words, 45 out of 50 respondents answer Strongly Agree on your survey item) then you should add more points to your scale. This will improve the variability of responses to your survey statement, which will help you to find out why people think both positively and negatively toward a particular criminal justice issue. Remember this simple rule: *The greater the number of points in your Likert scale, the greater the variability in your responses.*

RESPONSES TO DIFFICULT QUESTIONS

Many criminal justice surveys deal with sensitive issues. When a Likert scale is used on these surveys, people tend to pick "Neither agree nor disagree" as their preferred answer. This is because, for whatever reason, they do not wish to express their true opinions. There is a way around this problem, however: the **ranked response** technique.

To use a ranked response, simply ask respondents to rank a set of responses from high to low, most preferred to least preferred, and so on, as in this example:

> As a police officer, which of the following community relations techniques do you have the most difficulty carrying out on a day-to-day basis? Please rank the following categories from 1 (the most difficult for you to do) to 5 (the least difficult for you to do).
>
> _____ Being a good listener to citizens
>
> _____ Understanding citizens' problems
>
> _____ Being helpful in solving citizens' problems
>
> _____ Being polite when citizens are rude
>
> _____ Caring about citizens' needs

Responses to this question will indicate which community relations techniques are most and least difficult for officers, without necessarily requiring the officers to say, "I have a problem."

Always bear in mind, however, that ranking responses can be confusing to respondents. Therefore, instructions for ranked response questions must be clear and should provide examples of how to answer the question (when possible). Also, try to keep the number of responses that are being ranked to a minimum. It is best to limit the number of ranked responses to five or fewer items.

EXERCISES

MULTIPLE CHOICE: SURVEY ANSWERS

Read each statement carefully, then choose the word or phrase that correctly completes the statement.

1. A survey question that asks for the answer to be written in by the respondent is
    a. closed-ended
    b. open-ended
    c. mutually exclusive
    d. exhaustive   _____

2. Survey questions that provide a selection of answers are
    a. closed-ended
    b. open-ended
    c. mutually exclusive
    d. exhaustive   _____

3. If a closed-ended survey question does not contain all possible responses to a question or statement, the question is not
    a. mutually exclusive
    b. exhaustive
    c. scaled
    d. ranked   _____

4. Survey answers including categories that do not overlap with one another are
    a. mutually exclusive
    b. exhaustive
    c. open-ended
    d. sensitive   _____

5. The word *other* is used in survey answers to guard against problems resulting from lack of
    a. mutual exclusiveness
    b. exhaustiveness

    c. scaling

    d. ranking   _____

6. Responses to survey questions that are ranked from *strongly agree* to *strongly disagree* are

    a. open-ended

    b. Likert scales

    c. not exhaustive

    d. not mutually exclusive   _____

7. If a Likert scale survey response lacks variability, the scale should be changed by

    a. adding more points

    b. taking away points

    c. lengthening the question

    d. reducing the question   _____

8. If a survey question asks for sensitive or embarrassing information, it is best to make the response

    a. closed-ended

    b. open-ended

    c. scaled

    d. exhaustive   _____

9. Responses to survey questions that measure degrees of difference are

    a. scaled

    b. ranked

    c. sensitive

    d. unmeasureable   _____

10. The ranked response technique is helpful for getting information from respondents who are answering

    a. sensitive questions

    b. scaled questions

    c. experimental questions

    d. both a and b   _____

IDENTIFICATION MATCH: SURVEY ANSWERS

Each of the following statements describes a method or characteristic of survey answers. Using the key provided, match each statement with the correct method or characteristic.

Key:
OE = open-ended
CE = closed-ended
ME = mutually exclusive
EX = exhaustive

_____ 1. Type of survey answer used most often in criminal justice research

_____ 2. Problem created when *fairly satisfied* and *fairly dissatisfied* are responses to the same question

_____ 3. A problem that is evident when a large number of respondents choose the category *other*

_____ 4. Survey answer type with categories *yes* and *no*

_____ 5. A type of survey question that requires the researcher to make judgement calls or interpretations about the respondent's answer

_____ 6. Answers to survey questions that could be placed in one or more categories

_____ 7. The best type of survey answer for asking questions about "crimes that a respondent has committed"

_____ 8. A survey question with a five-point Likert scale response

_____ 9. A survey question requiring the respondent to answer by filling in his or her age

_____ 10. The type of survey question that is used least often in criminal justice research

MATCHING TEST: SURVEY ANSWERS

Insert the correct term or phrase after each definition.

open-ended   Likert scale
closed-ended   ranked response
exhaustive   other
mutually exclusive points

1. Used to create variability in Likert scales

_____

2. Question type whose answer is circled or filled in by the respondent

_____

3. Question type whose answer is written in by the respondent

_____

4. A word used to detect problems with exhaustiveness

_____

5. A survey answer that contains all possible responses

_____

6. The answers range from high to low

_____

7. The most common type of closed-ended question used in criminal justice research

_____

8. Categories of answers to survey questions that are clearly distinct from one another

_____

9. Usually added to Likert scale responses that lack variability

_____

10. Survey answers that measure degrees of difference in attitudes, opinions, and feelings

SHORT ANSWER TEST: SURVEY ANSWERS

Answer each of the following questions in the space provided.

1. Explain when and under what circumstances it is best to use a closed-ended and an open-ended response.

   _____

   _____

   _____

   _____

   _____

   _____

   _____

   _____

   _____

   _____

2. Explain what is meant by the terms *mutually exclusive* and *exhaustive* with respect to wording responses to survey questions.

   _____

   _____

   _____

   _____

   _____

   _____

   _____

   _____

   _____

3. Construct Likert items with three-, five-, and nine-point scale responses (for a total of three Likert items).

_____

_____

_____

_____

_____

_____

_____

_____

_____

_____

4. Construct two survey questions related to a criminal justice topic that contain mutually exclusive and exhaustive closed-ended response categories (that are not Likert scales).

_____

_____

_____

_____

_____

_____

_____

_____

_____

_____

_____

_____

11

Surveys, Part III: Putting Criminal Justice Surveys Together

LEARNING OBJECTIVE

To determine the proper placement and ordering of questions, sections, and subsections of the criminal justice survey instrument.

KEY LEARNING POINTS

TYPES OF SURVEYS

Surveys come in many forms. What you are probably used to seeing is the standard **self-administered survey.** Briefly, a self-administered survey is simply a survey that comes with its own set of instructions; a respondent simply reads it and completes it. This type of survey has definite advantages for criminal justice applications because it is inexpensive to administer and it usually does not take a long time to construct.

Another type of survey is the **interview schedule.** Unlike self-administered surveys, interview schedules are surveys that are administered verbally to people by an interviewer. As you can imagine, this method is much more time-consuming and expensive than merely handing out surveys to a group of people to complete. However, the interview schedule has distinct advantages over other methods in that it usually has a very high response rate.

Response rates, or the number of people who actually complete a survey, tend to be very low in self-administered surveys (in most cases between 20 and 40 percent). Interview schedules, on the other hand, have response rates of around 80 percent. Remember that a good response rate is essential for demonstrating the accuracy of the data obtained from surveys.

GROUP QUESTIONS ACCORDING TO COMMON THEMES

The first step in putting together your criminal justice survey is to group your questions according to **common themes.** Obviously, themes that you create can be either broad or narrow. However, it is best to keep your themes as narrow as possible in order to keep your respondents focused on the topic the questions are addressing. Theme categories that contain too many questions, or are too broad, will cause the people reading your survey to tire quickly when answering your questions. When this happens, the quality of the data goes down dramatically.

The individual theme categories should be offset with some type of line or border, and each one should include its own set of descriptions or instructions, as in the following example:

YOUR INTEREST IN POLICE WORK

To begin, we would like to know about your interests, background, and motivation in police work.

1. What was the primary reason for your becoming a police officer?
   [ ] job security
   [ ] to provide a needed service
   [ ] excitement
   [ ] salary
   [ ] other _____

ORDERING QUESTIONS WITHIN THEMES

Now that you have your questions grouped by themes, you must order them within the theme categories. There are a few rules to remember. First, it is best to put any sensitive questions at the end of the section. This is a very important point to remember when asking questions such as "Have you ever committed a crime?" or "Have you ever been the victim of a crime?" Questions that may cause emotional reactions are best asked **after** other, less emotional questions have been asked. If sensitive questions are asked at the beginning of a theme category, chances are they will not be answered, and they may even prevent the respondent from answering any of the questions in the entire theme category.

The second rule concerns question length. It is best to put shorter questions at the beginning of the theme section. Starting a section with long questions may cause the respondent to skip an entire block of questions because answering them simply looks like too much work. Remember, if a question is too long it should be reworded into a shorter version.

Finally, and perhaps most important, question ordering should always follow the **specific to the general** rule. If your goal is to get an overall opinion as well as specifics about something, put the specific questions before the overall opinion question. For example, suppose you are constructing a survey for cadets who have just graduated from the police academy, and you want to find out how they feel about their academy training. It would not be wise to ask the question, "Overall, what is your opinion of your academy training?" before asking specific opinion questions about academy experiences such as driving training, weapons training, legal training, and so forth. The reason: An overall opinion will bias subsequent opinions on specific questions. On the other hand, specific questions that come before a general question will cause the respondent to think through many factors prior to answering the general opinion question. The following example demonstrates this question ordering principle:

Sample Question

Overall, how would you rate your academy training in the following areas?

	Excellent	Good	Fair	Poor
Physical	[ ]	[ ]	[ ]	[ ]
Defense tactics	[ ]	[ ]	[ ]	[ ]
Stress	[ ]	[ ]	[ ]	[ ]
Education	[ ]	[ ]	[ ]	[ ]
Firearms	[ ]	[ ]	[ ]	[ ]
First aid	[ ]	[ ]	[ ]	[ ]
Driving	[ ]	[ ]	[ ]	[ ]
Reports	[ ]	[ ]	[ ]	[ ]

How would you rate your overall satisfaction with your academy training?

[ ] extremely satisfied   [ ] satisfied

[ ] unsatisfied   [ ] extremely unsatisfied

THE ORDERING OF THEME CATEGORIES

Now that you have your questions organized into themes as well as within themes, you have to organize the overall survey. The general rule is the same as that for organizing your questions within themes. That is, place shorter, less sensitive themes at the beginning of the questionnaire and longer or more sensitive themes at the end. Also, if there is a logical flow from one theme to another, by all means follow it!

A special note on demographics. Demographic questions are included in almost every survey. They include questions regarding the respondents' background characteristics such as age, ethnicity, gender, educational level, marital status, and household income. The purpose of demographic questions is to generate variables that can be used to group respondents into roughly equal background and social class categories when making statistical comparisons. (See What about Statistical Controls? in Module 8 for a related discussion.) Demographic variables are also necessary for developing a statistical profile of your respondents; that is, describing their average age, income, and so forth.

For many respondents, providing demographic information is bothersome and a sensitive issue. Many people consider it an invasion of their privacy to provide researchers with personal information about their backgrounds and household. Therefore, demographic questions should be considered sensitive and placed at the end of the survey instrument.

THE OVERALL APPEARANCE

When you have completely arranged the questions and themes in your survey, the overall appearance should be **uncluttered.** Don't make the type too small or try to put too much on a page. If your survey looks crammed in or cluttered it will not adjust appeal to those who have to read and answer it, and your response rate will suffer dramatically.

METHODS THAT SAVE SPACE

You can save considerable space in your survey by **blocking** certain groups of questions. Questions can be blocked when they share the same theme and the same response categories. To block questions, simply group the questions and their response categories as in this example:

Please tell us how good a job the police are doing in your neighborhood as far as . . .

	Satisfactory Job	Unsatisfactory Job
1. Preventing Accidents	[ ]	[ ]
2. Controlling Traffic	[ ]	[ ]
3. Handling Gangs	[ ]	[ ]
4. Preventing Crime	[ ]	[ ]

FILTERING QUESTIONS

You can save your respondents considerable time and perhaps increase their willingness to complete your entire survey by **filtering** questions. Filtering questions generally helps respondents to skip to specific sets of questions that pertain to them. The following questions illustrate this technique:

7. Did you receive any pre-academy training?

    ┌────[ ] yes   [ ] no (skip to question 10)
    ↓

7a. What type of training? _____

7b. How helpful was this training in preparing you for the academy?

[ ] extremely helpful [ ] helpful

[ ] not helpful [ ] extremely unhelpful

EXERCISES

MULTIPLE CHOICE TEST: PUTTING SURVEYS TOGETHER

Read each statement carefully, then choose the word or phrase that correctly completes the statement.

1. After questions, statements, and answers have been written, they should be arranged in the survey according to
   a. theory
   b. common themes
   c. randomness
   d. hypotheses   _____

2. The number of respondents who actually complete and return usable surveys represents the
   a. respondent count
   b. sample estimate
   c. response rate
   d. sample size   _____

3. If researchers ask questions concerning the respondents' personal background, such as age, ethnicity, or level of education, this information is called
   a. baseline data
   b. demographic data
   c. fill data
   d. safety data   _____

4. When questions are grouped together and given a common set of closed-ended responses, these questions are
   a. block questions
   b. filter questions
   c. contingency questions
   d. rated questions   _____

5. A survey conducted with a respondent over the telephone is an example of a (an)
   a. self-administered survey
   b. mail survey

  c. interview schedule

  d. both a and b   _____

6. When a general question is included within a common theme category, this question should be placed

  a. before specific questions

  b. after specific questions

  c. outside the theme

  d. in another theme   _____

7. In order to create the appearance of being quick and easy to complete, you should make your survey look

  a. full

  b. large

  c. uncluttered

  d. cluttered   _____

8. When a survey includes a series of specific questions that may not be answered by all respondents, these questions should be preceded by a

  a. block question

  b. filtering question

  c. contingency question

  d. random question   _____

9. A survey that is mailed to respondents is an example of a (an)

  a. interview schedule

  b. self-administered survey

  c. telephone survey

  d. audible survey   _____

10. Theme categories containing questions that are sensitive or embarrassing should be

  a. excluded from the survey

  b. placed at the end of the survey

  c. given in a separate survey

  d. self-administered   _____

IDENTIFICATION MATCH: PUTTING SURVEYS TOGETHER

Each of the following statements describes a characteristic of a survey. Using the key provided, indicate whether or not the survey was well put together.

Key:
WP = well constructed
NP = not well constructed

_____ 1. Demographic questions placed at the beginning of a survey

_____ 2. Theme categories that contain several issues or topics

_____ 3. Specific questions come before a general question

_____ 4. Sensitive questions placed at the end of a theme category

_____ 5. Survey forms with wide margins and small fonts or type

_____ 6. Blocking questions that have the same response categories

_____ 7. Filtering questions that may not apply to all respondents

_____ 8. Using interview schedules when time and money are in short supply

_____ 9. Using a self-administered survey when the desired response rate is 80 percent

_____ 10. Sensitive questions placed at the end of the survey

MATCHING TEST: PUTTING SURVEYS TOGETHER

Insert the correct term or phrase after each definition.

self-administered   filtering question
interview schedule   response rate
theme categories   uncluttered
specific to general   block questions
within theme categories   demographics

1. Background characteristics of the respondent

2. The number of respondents who complete a survey

3. The method of organizing questions within themes

4. Survey administered and completed by the respondent

5. Survey answered verbally by the respondent

6. The method of grouping questions by response category

7. The method of using one question to screen out others

8. Used to group questions that relate to a common topic

9. The second step after organizing questions into themes

10. How the survey should appear to the respondent

SHORT ANSWER TEST: PUTTING SURVEYS TOGETHER

Answer each of the following questions in the space provided.

1. What benefits are obtained for the researcher by placing questions into common themes rather than placing questions at random in a survey?

_____

_____

_____

_____

2. What is likely to happen if sensitive or embarrassing questions are placed at the beginning of a theme section or survey instrument?

_____

_____

_____

_____

_____

_____

3. Write ten separate survey questions and arrange them into common themes. Also, within one of the themes, illustrate the specific to general rule.

_____

_____

_____

_____

_____

_____

_____

_____

_____

_____

_____

_____

NAME

12
Surveys, Part IV: Completing and Distributing Surveys

LEARNING OBJECTIVE

To identify important factors in the marketing of survey instruments to potential respondents and to become familiar with techniques used to track and assess survey response patterns.

KEY LEARNING POINTS

PACKAGING THE SURVEY

Surveys must be interesting and appealing or they will not be completed and returned. If they are not returned, your response rate may be so low that you will be unable to draw accurate conclusions from the small number of surveys that have been returned. Therefore, it is important to effectively market your survey to the audience for which it is intended. There are several things that can be done to improve a survey's audience appeal.

Visual appeal. Survey instruments that have very small type or too many questions packed on one page lack **visual appeal**, and they rarely get returned because people think it will take a great deal of time and effort to complete them. Thus, at first glance, your survey should give the appearance that it can be completed easily. The best way to ensure the visual appeal of your survey instrument is to:

1. Arrange questions on pages so that the pages look open and uncluttered. Use wide margins and avoid small type.
2. Limit the number of pages by using two-sided page duplication and eliminating unnecessary questions.
3. Make liberal use of block question formats to save space.

Cover letter. The **cover letter** is attached to the outside of your survey (or sometimes copied onto the first page of the survey) and serves to introduce the researcher and the objective of the research to the audience (i.e., the future respondents). The cover letter is important because it will sell your survey to the audience. Whether or not a person decides to even look at your survey instrument depends on the effectiveness of the cover letter. Here are some tips on how to write a good cover letter:

1. Don't write a long letter. Try to keep it to two or three paragraphs.
2. Address the Who, What, Where, Why, and How in the letter:
   - Who is conducting the research (i.e., the research staff)?
   - What is being done?
   - Where is the research being carried out?
   - Why is the research being conducted?
   - How is the research being performed?
3. Emphasize how the research will be of benefit to the respondent.

4. Include contact information that can be used by the respondent to gain further information regarding the research project.

DISTRIBUTING THE SURVEY

Most criminal justice surveys are either hand delivered (i.e., handed out in person by the researcher) or mailed. Because hand delivered surveys are usually given to a captive audience, they tend to have much higher return rates than surveys that have been mailed out. It is not uncommon to have low return rates (between 20 and 30 percent) on a mailed survey. Therefore, it is important to use every possible method to improve the return rate of mailed-out surveys. Here are some pointers:

1. *Envelope addressing.* Make the mailing envelope as personal and nonbusiness looking as possible. When possible, avoid using computer-generated mailing labels. Handwritten envelopes have the best odds of being opened.

2. *Mailing.* Try not to use metered postage; use a stamp instead. Most people associate metered postage with junk mail. It is always a good idea, if you can afford it, to send surveys by first-class mail. First-class mail is forwarded to new addresses and this will help to ensure that the survey reaches the respondent. You can save money by using a first-class pre-sort stamp. It is less expensive than regular first-class postage, but requires that you group your mailing envelopes by common zip codes.

3. *Include an SASE.* SASE stands for Self-Addressed Stamped Envelope. You should include an SASE for respondents to use in returning the survey. Never assume that respondents will return a survey using their own postage.

4. *Make a return list.* To keep track of who has returned surveys and who has not, it is important to create a return list. This can be done in several ways, but should never

cause the respondent to think he or she is being personally identified. Most often, some sort of code number is marked on the SASE that corresponds to the respondent's mailing address.

POSTING YOUR SURVEY RETURNS

Expect to get the bulk of your returns (approximately 80 percent) within the first two weeks after mailing out your survey. If your return rate seems abnormally low in the first two weeks after mailing, don't expect it to improve in the weeks to come.

The best way to improve a poor return rate is to do a **survey follow-up.** Survey follow-ups simply involve making contact with the respondents who have not returned the survey and persuading them to complete it (or a new survey). It should be easy to find out who did not return their surveys by examining your return list. Follow-up contact with respondents can be made either by phone (when phone numbers are available) or by mail. When following-up by mail, include a brief letter explaining that a first survey was sent and that you are anticipating a return. Also include in the follow-up mailing a new cover letter and survey, in case the respondent lost or misplaced the original survey.

A NOTE ON RESPONSE ERROR

The accuracy of survey information depends on who the respondents are. It is not always important that you have a high return rate (although this is very helpful); however, it is important to find out if the lack of response is evenly distributed among different groups of people. When a particular group of respondents fails to return your survey, their input or opinions will not be counted in the big picture. This could cause your survey results to suffer from **response error.**

Response error is dangerous because it can distort the big picture of your survey findings. For example, suppose you hand your survey out to a large police department with the intention of finding out how well the average officer likes his or her job. Also suppose almost all veteran officers in the department return their surveys, while only a small fraction of rookie officers return theirs. Finally, suppose you average the responses to your survey and find out that 90 percent of all officers say that they "love their job" in the police department. Might the percentage of officers who state that they love their job change if the rookies had provided more responses to the survey? If you think it would, then these particular survey results suffer from response error.

To determine if a survey suffers from response error, you need to find out if specific groups of people with low response rates think or feel differently from those who did respond. This can be done by contacting a small portion of the nonresponding group, perhaps by phone or in person, and asking them to complete key sections of the survey where you suspect response error exists.

Another way to detect response error is to track late responses. More often than not, people who respond late (e.g., more than two weeks after mailing) tend to think very much like those who do not respond at all. Thus, it is possible to detect response error by comparing survey responses between late and timely respondents.

EXERCISES

MULTIPLE CHOICE TEST: COMPLETING SURVEYS

Read each statement carefully, then choose the word or phrase that correctly completes the statement.

1. Surveys that lack visual appeal are
   a. more likely returned
   b. less likely returned
   c. uncluttered
   d. both a and c   _____

2. Which of the following is not a method of increasing the visual appeal of surveys?
   a. open pages
   b. two-sided page duplication
   c. use of block questions
   d. use of small type   _____

3. The most important factor in selling your survey to its audience is
   a. packaging
   b. visual appeal
   c. the cover letter
   d. distribution method   _____

4. The length of a cover letter should not exceed
   a. two sentences
   b. three sentences
   c. two or three paragraphs
   d. two or three pages   _____

5. To keep track of survey returns, it is important to use
   a. metered postage
   b. an SASE
   c. a return list
   d. handwritten envelopes   _____

6. Which of the following should be avoided when addressing envelopes for mailed-out surveys?
   a. handwritten addresses
   b. nonbusiness appearance
   c. personal appearance
   d. computer labels _____

7. Which of the following mailing methods is recommended for sending out mailed surveys?
   a. metered postage
   b. second-class postage
   c. pre-sort, first class
   d. regular first class _____

8. After surveys are mailed to respondents, the bulk of survey returns are generally received within
   a. one week
   b. two weeks
   c. three weeks
   d. one month _____

9. The best way to improve a survey's poor return rate is to do a
   a. survey follow-up
   b. response tracking
   c. postsurvey
   d. second survey _____

10. Response error is likely to be highest when the number of surveys completed and returned is
    a. high
    b. about average
    c. low
    d. extremely high _____

IDENTIFICATION MATCH: COMPLETING SURVEYS

Each of the following statements relates to the distribution and completion of surveys. Using the key provided, match each statement with the correct word or phrase.

Key:
VA = visual appeal
CL = cover letter
DI = distribution
RE = response error
PO = posting returns

_____ 1. An envelope that is personal and nonbusiness-like

_____ 2. Making contact with respondents who have not returned surveys

_____ 3. Including an SASE with the survey

_____ 4. Arranging questions so that survey pages look open

_____ 5. Using a first-class, pre-sort stamp

_____ 6. It can distort the big picture of your survey findings

_____ 7. Telling the respondents the who, what, where, why, and how of the proposed research

_____ 8. Recontacting respondents either by phone or by mail

_____ 9. Specific groups who think differently and do not complete and return the survey

_____ 10. Use wide margins and avoid small type on survey forms

NAME

MATCHING TEST: COMPLETING SURVEYS

Insert the correct term or phrase after each definition.

packaging   survey distribution
visual appeal   survey returns
cover letter   follow-up
response error   SASE

1. Methods of making your survey interesting and appealing

_____

2. Serves to introduce the research objective to respondents

_____

3. Stands for self-addressed, stamped envelope

_____

4. Detected by contacting persons not returning a survey

_____

5. About 80 percent are received within two weeks of first mailing

_____

6. Making a survey appear easy to complete

_____

7. Best way to improve a low survey response rate

_____

8. Methods to improve the return rate of mailed surveys

_____

SHORT ANSWER TEST: COMPLETING SURVEYS

Answer each of the following questions in the space provided.

1. Explain some methods that can be used to make your survey more appealing to its audience.

_____

_____

_____

_____

_____

_____

2. What is response error? What are some of the ways response error can be detected and dealt with by the researcher?

_____

_____

_____

_____

_____

_____

_____

3. In the space below, write a complete cover letter for a survey that concerns a criminal justice topic of your choice.

_____

_____

_____

_____

_____

_____

_____

NAME

Sampling

LEARNING OBJECTIVE

To understand the relationship between probability and nonprobability sampling methods, and to understand how to carry out these methods in applied criminal justice settings.

KEY LEARNING CONCEPTS

INTRODUCTION TO SAMPLING

Sampling, in many ways, is the most important step in the criminal justice research process. This is true because sampling is the procedure used to gather the people, places, or things that you are going to study. The old saying—garbage in, garbage out—is appropriate here. When you gather a sample that is less than adequate, you run the risk of drawing research conclusions from this sample that are biased and inaccurate. A research study is only as good as the sample foundation it is based on.

WHAT IS A SAMPLE?

A **sample** is simply any subset or smaller group of people, places, or things that is taken from a larger group of people, places, or things. It is the sample that the researcher studies and bases research conclusions on. For example, if you are interested in studying state judges, you might decide to study a sample of 15 judges who represent the entire group of judges serving the state.

WHAT IS A POPULATION?

While the sample refers to a smaller group taken from a larger group, the term **population** refers to the larger group from which the sample (or smaller group) is taken. Before gathering a sample, it is important to identify your population. The population includes every person, place, or object from which you draw your sample. In the example above, all judges serving the state would be the study population.

PROBABILITY SAMPLING AND NONPROBABILITY SAMPLING

Most criminal justice research relies on **probability samples.** Probability samples allow the researcher to draw conclusions and make predictions about a particular population by studying the sample. On the other hand, **nonprobability samples** are merely samples drawn from a population that do not allow conclusions or predictions to be made about the population. The primary difference between these two sampling methods is in the way the samples are drawn from the population.

RANDOM SELECTION AND PROBABILITY SAMPLING

If the aim of your study is to draw conclusions about a population by studying a sample from that population (most often the case in criminal justice research), you will need to use probability sampling. The key step in drawing a probability sample is known as **random selection.** Something is randomly selected when every single person, place, or thing in the population has an equal chance of being selected.

There are certain methods that guarantee that samples are randomly selected in a proper manner. However, your selection process need not be complex. To the contrary, flipping a coin or drawing names in lottery style are perfectly acceptable methods for ensuring random selection. But you must always make sure that every single element or member of your population is included in the selection process.

METHODS OF PROBABILITY SAMPLING

1. Simple random sampling. As the name implies, this method is simple because it requires nothing more than a clearly defined population and the random selection of people, places, or things from this population (by lottery, coin toss, or other true random method). However, this method does have its limitations, especially when populations are extremely large. For example, suppose you were conducting a citizen attitude survey of an entire city (with a population of, say, 100,000). Even if you put all of the names and addresses of residents in a hat and draw a sample, your sample would be spread throughout the entire city. This would present a problem if you were conducting face-to-face interviews within neighborhoods.

Even more important, the **simple random sample** tends to distort certain groups within populations when the sample size is small relative to the population size. To illustrate this limitation, assume that you are studying the height of new recruits in a large police academy. The police academy has 1,000 new recruits and you draw a simple random sample of 10 percent, or 100 of these recruits. From this sample, you discover that the average height in your sample of 100 recruits is 5'10" (allowing for a small degree of error).

There might be a problem with your results if the number of male and female officers in the population of 1,000 recruits is considered. Let's assume that out of the 1,000 recruits, 100 (or 10 percent) are female and the remainder (900 or 90 percent) are male. The simple random sampling method should have provided us with a sample that contains approximately 10 females and 90 males, reflecting the gender breakdown in the population. However, more often than not, simple random sampling fails to do this. Instead, it is usually the case that simple random sampling causes larger groups within a population (such as the male recruits in this example) to be overrepresented in the sample. In our example, if simple random sampling caused males to be overrepresented in the recruit sample, this would probably cause the 5'10" estimate to be higher than the true average height of all recruits in the population (assuming the female recruits are not as tall as the male recruits). There are other sampling methods that are better equipped to deal with these situations.

2. Stratified sampling. Stratified sampling involves breaking the population into sections, or strata, and then simply randomly selecting sample subjects from each of these sections or strata. Stratified sampling offers an easy solution to the sampling problem encountered in the police academy example. It can be carried out through the following steps:

A. *Identify the strata of interest in the population.*
    EXAMPLE: In the present case they will be officer gender, with two levels: male officers and female officers.

B. *Determine the percentage of male and female officers in the population. You need to do this because you want to match the percentages of males and females in the sample to those in the population.*
    EXAMPLE: You know that there are 1,000 officers in the population, 900 males and 100 females. Therefore, converting these figures to percentages we find: 900/1,000=.09 and .09 × 100=90% males, with the remaining 10% being females.

C. *Determine how large of a sample you want to draw (say 10% of the population) and then calculate the number of males and females you must select according to the percentages of males and females in the population.*
    EXAMPLE: In this example, we want to draw a 10 percent sample, consisting of 100 persons (1,000 × .10=100).

Then, if our sample consists of 100 persons, we must select 90 males (100 × .90=90 or 90% of the sample) and 10 females (100 × .10=10%) to exactly reproduce the percentages of males and females in the original population of officers.

D. *Randomly select subjects within the strata.*

EXAMPLE: To complete the stratified sample, randomly select 90 male and 10 female officers from the population.

Unlike simple random sampling, the stratified sample will directly reproduce the number of male and female officers in the original population. Thus, we minimize the chance of error or bias due to over- or undercounting males and females when we draw conclusions about the population of officers from the stratified sample.

3. Systematic sampling. Systematic sampling is a very convenient method that is often used in real-world criminal justice research applications. Some people call this method interval sampling because it involves drawing a sample of subjects from a population using predetermined intervals. It is typically carried out as follows:

A. *Determine the percentage sample that you want to draw from the population, e.g., 10 percent, 20 percent, and so forth.*

EXAMPLE: Again, suppose we have a population of 1,000 police academy recruits and we want to draw a 10 percent sample (100 recruits).

B. *Determine the systematic sampling interval based on the number of subjects you want to draw from the population.*

EXAMPLE: To determine the **sampling interval,** simply divide the desired number of subjects by the population size. In this case, 100/1,000= an interval size of 10.

C. *Select sample subjects from the population at the prescribed interval, using the entire population.*

EXAMPLE: You will probably have a list or sampling frame from which to draw your sample. From our list of 1,000 recruits, we would begin at the top of the list and select our first sample subject from the tenth place on the list, our second from the twentieth place on the list, and so on until we reached the bottom of the list. This would create a final sample of 100 recruits.

Systematic sampling is easy to use if you have a list of the population and the list is not too long. The important thing to remember about systematic sampling is that you must use the entire list or the final sample will not be randomly selected. For example, suppose we had a huge list of academy recruits (say 10,000 from several states) that consisted of 100 pages of names. Could we start at the beginning of the list and select our subjects from the first ten pages of the list? The answer is no, because the first few pages of the list may not be random. What if this list was arranged by age or gender? Then sampling from the first set of pages would create a sample that consisted of all older officers or male officers or vice versa. As you can see from this example, you must always sample from the entire population when using systematic sampling.

SAMPLE SIZE

How large does a sample have to be? This is a very difficult question to answer. Most often, the size of your sample will be determined by practical factors such as the time and resources allowed to perform the research. If you are conducting survey research, remember that there will be a relatively high nonresponse rate, so you will have to sample far more respondents than you intend to study. There are complex statistical formulas that can be used to estimate an appropriate sample size given a specific research task. But the bottom line is practicality. Ask yourself, given the number of research questions that are being asked and the number of variables that are being investigated, what number of subjects or respondents is sufficient. In answering this question, remember that the greater the differences that exist in your population (that is, the greater the variability), the larger your sample will have to be to capture those differences.

EXERCISES

Read each statement carefully, then choose the word or phrase that correctly completes the statement.

1. The larger group from which a sample is taken is known as the
   a. universe
   b. subsample
   c. population
   d. element _____

2. Which type of sampling involves breaking the sample into sections?
   a. simple random
   b. stratified
   c. cluster
   d. systematic _____

3. Samples are drawn from a list called a
   a. sampling roster
   b. sampling frame
   c. sampling file
   d. sampling list _____

4. Every single element in a population has an equal probability of being included in a sample when using
   a. nonprobability
   b. purposive sampling
   c. random assignment
   d. random selection _____

5. The sampling method used most often in real-world criminal justice research applications is
   a. systematic
   b. stratified
   c. nonprobability
   d. cluster _____

6. If a researcher selects every fifth judge from a sampling frame consisting of 200 judges, the final sample size will be
   a. 20
   b. 40
   c. 60
   d. 80 _____

7. If a population of 1,000 prison inmates consists of 200 violent inmates and 800 nonviolent inmates, then the number of violent inmates a researcher would have to randomly select to complete a 10 percent stratified sample is
   a. 20
   b. 200
   c. 250
   d. 500 _____

8. The type of sampling used by criminal justice researchers who want to draw conclusions about a particular population is
   a. nonprobability
   b. probability
   c. purposive
   d. snowball _____

9. Which of the following methods would result in the selection of a nonprobability sample?
   a. simple random sampling
   b. stratified sampling
   c. systematic sampling
   d. nonrandom sampling _____

10. The type of sampling that tends to distort certain groups within the population when the sample size is small is called
    a. simple random
    b. systematic
    c. stratified
    d. probability _____

IDENTIFICATION MATCH: SAMPLING

Each of the following statements describes a different sampling method. Using the key provided, match each statement with the sampling method it best describes.

Key:
SR = simple random
ST = stratified sampling
SY = systematic sampling
NP = nonprobability sampling

_____ 1. A sample drawn by taking names from a hat

_____ 2. A sample drawn by taking the first name from every page in a phone book

_____ 3. A sample drawn by picking out typical criminals from a jail

_____ 4. A sample drawn by the flip of a coin

_____ 5. A sample drawn by dialing random numbers on a telephone

_____ 6. A sample drawn by placing a survey on the Internet and asking people to respond by computer

_____ 7. A sample drawn by going into a room and asking for volunteers

_____ 8. A sample drawn by taking every fifth name from a sampling frame

_____ 9. A sample drawn by randomly selecting within variable subgroups

_____ 10. A sample drawn by selecting every name on the first page of a phone book

MATCHING TEST: SAMPLING

Insert the correct term or phrase after each definition.

sample	random selection
population	stratified sampling
probability sampling	systematic sampling
nonprobability sampling	simple random sampling
sampling frame	sampling interval

1. A smaller group or subset taken from a larger group

   _____

2. A sample that is not drawn by random selection

   _____

3. A sample drawn by random selection from a population

   _____

4. Drawing a sample at random within variable subsets

   _____

5. A larger group from which a sample is drawn

   _____

6. A list from which a sample is drawn

   _____

7. The number of cases used to select a systematic sample

   _____

8. The method used to ensure the drawing of a probability sample

   _____

9. Sampling that allows predictions about a population

   _____

10. A sampling method that involves the use of intervals

   _____

SHORT ANSWER TEST: SAMPLING

Answer each of the following questions in the space provided.

1. What are the basic differences between a sample and a population?

   _____

   _____

   _____

_____

_____

_____

_____

2. What is random selection and why is it important in the creation of a probability sample?

_____

_____

_____

_____

_____

_____

_____

3. You have been hired as a sampling consultant to the Bigcity Police Department. The department has 5,000 officers and it is your job to draw a 10 percent probability sample of these officers. The department's administration is interested in finding out how all of Bigcity's officers feel about a new, more restrictive use of force policy. The department has 4,500 veteran officers with over 10 years of experience and 500 rookie officers with under 10 years of experience. Explain how you would draw samples using simple random, stratified, and systematic sampling. When appropriate, give numeric examples (i.e., show how you obtained your numbers). Also, explain why one method might produce better results than another.

_____

_____

_____

_____

NAME
_____

NAME

14
MODULE

Conducting Ethical Criminal Justice Research

LEARNING OBJECTIVE

To understand and apply the legal, moral, and ethical obligations of performing criminal justice research.

KEY LEARNING POINTS

ETHICS AND THE OBJECTIVES OF CRIMINAL JUSTICE RESEARCH

The ultimate objective of criminal justice research is to seek the truth about and find solutions for problems confronting the criminal justice system. Although there are many ways to seek answers to these problems, the essence of practicing criminal justice research is to use science in an ethical manner. Criminal justice research is considered ethical when it is performed and reported in an honest way, without posing psychological or physical risks (or any other potentially harmful effects) to those who are participating in the research study.

THE PRINCIPLES OF ETHICAL CRIMINAL JUSTICE RESEARCH

The following standards have become widely accepted in the field of criminal justice for ensuring that research is conducted in an ethical manner.

1. Informed consent. It is important that you anticipate any and all possible negative effects that your criminal justice research may have on study participants. After that, it is your obligation as a criminal justice researcher to inform your subjects of these potential hazards or inconveniences resulting from participation in the research study. Sometimes these research risks are very subtle. For example, when police officers agree to provide information that is critical of their department's administration, and this information is published in a report, mere participation in the study might be professionally damaging to the officers involved. On a different note, suppose you were conducting a victimization survey that probed deeply into the circumstances surrounding victims' past violent encounters. This situation carries the potential for emotional trauma, and victims who participate in such a study should be warned of this danger.

People who give their consent to become research subjects must give consent without being forced or coerced in any way. That is, the person who is agreeing to participate in your study must not feel compelled or pressured to become a participant if he or she has reservations about doing so. Pressures to participate are often subtle. For example, inmates who are serving time in jails or prisons may think that by participating in a criminal justice study they will receive favors or be released early. By offering more than nominal pay for participation, researchers often push their subjects to do things in the name of research that they ordinarily might not do.

Consent should always be obtained in writing before involving your subjects in any aspect of research. The written consent does not have to be complicated. It should clearly state:

- Who is doing the research;
- When and where the research is being conducted;
- What is required of the research subject;
- What potential hazards, if any, may be encountered by the subject.

The consent form should be signed and dated by the subject in the presence of the researcher or another qualified witness. It should also contain a statement similar to this example:

> I have been informed and understand the personal and professional risks involved in participating in the above study. I agree to assume these risks, and my participation in this study is purely voluntary, without the promise of any special rewards from the research staff as the result of my participation.

Remember that the consent of minors to participate in criminal justice research must always be given by their parents or legal guardians.

2. Voluntary participation. Participation in any criminal justice research study should be strictly **voluntary.** It is important, especially when researching politically sensitive criminal justice issues, that research participants feel that they have a way out if they don't feel comfortable participating in your study. Often in criminal justice agencies that are based on a rank structure, persons of lower rank feel compelled to participate in a research study that is sponsored or initiated by higher-ranking persons such as supervisors or administrators. Make sure that criminal justice employees are participating in your study because they want to, not because they feel they have to out of a sense of duty. The quality of data obtained from true volunteers is always superior to that obtained from unwilling volunteers.

3. Anonymity. Anonymity refers to keeping the personal identities of your research subjects a secret. In the most strict sense of the word, anonymity can involve keeping the research subjects' identity a secret both from the public at large and from the researcher.

When possible, it is always a good idea to guarantee anonymity for your research subjects. Quite often, criminal justice issues involve personally and politically sensitive topics, and people are much more willing to discuss such issues when they know their names will not be associated with the research study.

4. Confidentiality. When researchers promise that their subjects' responses to a study will remain **confidential**, they are promising that research information will be presented in such a way that the subjects' individual opinions and ideas are not revealed. Because most criminal justice research is reported in the **aggregate** (that is, individual responses are grouped into averages), there is little need even for researchers to be concerned with the personal identities of those they study. Therefore, for maximum protection of your subjects' identities, it is recommended that a person's name never be associated in any way with surveys or any other type of response form. If you use numeric codes as substitutes for names, you can honestly say that you don't know the true identities of your research subjects.

5. Protecting against physical and psychological harm. Above all, you should always provide your research subjects with the maximum available protection against physical or psychological harm resulting from your research. If you are conducting research within an organizational or university setting, be sure to check on official procedures that are already in place for approving research studies. You may be required to have your research ideas approved by a Human Research Committee that reviews proposed research studies for potential harm to subjects. These committees are typically found in university settings, and are staffed by experts who can provide you with technical and legal assistance to make sure your study conforms to accepted ethical research standards.

A NOTE ON COVERT RESEARCH

It is generally considered unethical to perform research on a person or group of persons without first informing them of your research intentions. In other words, you should never perform what is known as **covert research.** Even at the risk of having people act differently because of the study, you should never involve subjects in a criminal justice research study without first telling them that you are a researcher and that they (your subjects) are under study.

EXERCISES

MULTIPLE CHOICE TEST: RESEARCH ETHICS

Read each statement carefully, then choose the word or phrase that correctly completes the statement.

1. When people give their consent to become research participants, their consent must not be
   a. paid for
   b. voluntary
   c. forced
   d. informed _____

2. Which of the following groups of persons must be given special consideration when obtaining consent to participate in criminal justice research?
   a. children
   b. jail inmates
   c. prison inmates
   d. all of these groups _____

3. Consent to participate in criminal justice research should always be obtained
   a. verbally
   b. in writing
   c. by telephone
   d. by a lawyer _____

4. Participation in any criminal justice research should be strictly
   a. voluntary
   b. involuntary
   c. without pay
   d. paid for _____

5. Keeping the personal identity of a research subject secret is called
   a. anonymity
   b. confidentiality

  c. covert research
  d. both a and b _____
6. Researchers promising not to present information provided by a subject in such a way that the subject's individual opinions or ideas are revealed are guaranteeing
  a. confidentiality
  b. anonymity
  c. voluntary participation
  d. informed consent _____
7. Reporting data in the aggregate means that the data are not reported
  a. individually
  b. in group form
  c. as averages
  d. in written form _____
8. Special groups or boards, often found at universities, that review proposed research studies for potential harm to research subjects are called
  a. Special Review Boards
  b. Research Review Boards
  c. Human Research Committees
  d. Protective Groups _____
9. Before conducting research, it is important that the researcher make sure that research subjects will be free from
  a. psychological harm
  b. physical harm
  c. media publicity
  d. both a and b _____
10. Performing research on a person or group of persons without first informing them of your research intentions is generally considered
  a. permissible
  b. unethical
  c. ethical
  d. good research _____

IDENTIFICATION MATCH: RESEARCH ETHICS

Each of the following statements describes either an ethical or an unethical research situation. Using the key provided, identify each research statement as ethical or unethical.

Key:
ET = ethical research
UN = unethical research

_____ 1. Reporting Sgt. Jones' comments about his supervisor

_____ 2. Obtaining written permission from a child's parents

_____ 3. Offering money to jail inmates to participate in a study

_____ 4. Telling someone she is under arrest to see her reaction

_____ 5. Having a police chief hand out a survey to all officers

_____ 6. Having prison guards hand out surveys to inmates to complete

_____ 7. Informing potential subjects of the potential hazards of research

_____ 8. Reporting the average level of job satisfaction for police officers

MATCHING TEST: RESEARCH ETHICS

Insert the correct term or phrase after each definition.

informed consent	aggregate
voluntary participation	psychological harm
anonymity	physical harm
confidentiality	covert research

1. Presenting subjects' information in the aggregate

2. Obtained by written permission forms

3. Participating in research without coercion or force

4. Injuries resulting from participating in a study

5. Stress or anxiety produced by research participation

6. Research conducted without the subject's knowledge

7. Not revealing the name of a research subject

8. Presenting research results in a grouped format

SHORT ANSWER TEST: RESEARCH ETHICS

Answer each of the following questions in the space provided.

1. Under what circumstances would a criminal justice research study be considered unethical?

_____

_____

_____

_____

_____

_____

_____

2. You are conducting a study of juveniles who have been sentenced to two days of community service for illegal possession of alcohol. You are especially interested in determining whether the experience of community service will persuade these juvenile offenders not to recommit their original crime. Compose a permission form that you might use to make sure that the juveniles' participation in your study is voluntary and informed. In doing so, you must anticipate possible negative effects on the juveniles who participate in the study.

_____

_____

_____

_____

_____

_____

_____

_____

_____

_____

_____

NAME

Research Abstracts

1. INTENSIVE PROBATION STUDY

This study examines the impact of a new, intensive probation program on high-risk probationers. A sample of 1,000 probationers was selected randomly, 500 of whom are violent offenders and 500 of whom are nonviolent offenders. All subjects were randomly assigned to either an intensive probation supervision group or a regular supervision group. At the end of a 12-month period, study results indicated that probationers assigned to the intensive supervision group were 30 percent less likely to have violated the conditions of their probation by committing a new crime. Thus, the general conclusion from this study is that the more closely probationers are supervised, the greater the chances are that they will successfully complete their probation.

2. INTERPERSONAL DISTANCE STUDY

This study examined the relationship of interpersonal distance between police officers and community members, and the willingness of community members to report criminal activities in their neighborhood. A target sample of 200 households was surveyed to determine 1) the level of personal familiarity with police officers who patrolled their neighborhood, and 2) whether or not any household member had been the victim of a crime within the last 12 months. Results from correlational analyses revealed that residents who were most familiar with the police in their neighborhood were also most likely to report their victimization to the police.

3. CLIMATE AND ASSAULTIVE BEHAVIOR STUDY

The following study investigates the relationship between climate and assaultive behavior. More specifically, we focus on the heat frustration hypothesis that states, "as the weather goes from warm to hot, the number of assaults will increase as the result of this weather change." Study data consisted of 15 years of weather information (gathered from the U.S. Weather Service) and assault statistics (gathered from the UCR) representing Phoenix, Arizona. Assault trends were analyzed in 1-month intervals over the 15-year study period. Study results indicated that assault rates were highest during the warmest months of the year, thus supporting the heat frustration hypothesis.

4. PRISON EXECUTION AND DEATH PENALTY STUDY

This study examines the impact of prison executions on attitudes toward the death penalty. The study was carried out by conducting telephone interviews with 500 retired prison guards regarding their feelings toward the death penalty (either positive or negative) both before and after an actual execution was held in California's San Quentin Prison. Study respondents were selected at random from a list of retired prison guards living in the San Francisco Bay Area (every tenth subject from the initial list of 5,000 was selected). Study results indicated that the majority of respondents shifted their attitudes to a less favorable opinion of the death penalty after the actual execution took place.

5. REPORTING MODE STUDY

This study investigates the impact of reporting mode on the willingness of citizens to report criminal behavior to police. Specifically, we examine whether persons witnessing a low-level crime would be more willing to report the crime if they were given a chance to contact police via computer rather than by telephone. Subjects participating in the study were 200 college students who were randomly assigned to two groups: one group who reported crimes via computer and the other group who reported crimes via the traditional 911 telephone method. Study results indicated that the group reporting crimes by computer was three times more likely to contact police, compared to the group reporting crime by telephone.

6. DRUNK DRIVING LAW STUDY

This study investigates the impact of a new drunk driving law that requires mandatory jail time for persons driving drunk on weekend nights. The study sample consisted of randomly selected persons who had previously been convicted of drunk driving. The sample was broken down into two groups: persons who had served jail time for their offenses and persons who had not served jail time. The sample was studied for one year before and after the new DUI law was imposed. Results indicated that, for both groups of subjects, the incidence of drunk driving violations was reduced significantly after the law was imposed.

7. PROSECUTING ATTORNEY STUDY

This study reports the results of a survey of prosecuting attorneys randomly selected from among the members of the American Bar Association. The survey measured the willingness of prosecutors to plea bargain in cases that carried very severe punishments. Results of the survey indicated that the more serious the sentence imposed for a crime, the more willing the prosecutors were to plea bargain.

8. POLICE PATROL STUDY

This study investigates the ability of police patrols to prevent criminal activity. The study was carried out by dividing the target city into three patrol zones: Zone 1, which had regular patrol activity; Zone 2, which had three times the regular patrol activity; and Zone 3, which had no police patrols at all. The location of each zone within the city was determined by random assignment. The study revealed no substantial crime differences among the three patrol zones.

9. DRIVE-BY SHOOTING STUDY

This study examines the ability of road closures to reduce drive-by shootings between rival gang members. Here, the general hypothesis was that "if the opportunities to make a quick getaway out of a rival gang neighborhood are reduced by blocking a number of entrances and exits into that neighborhood, then the number of drive-by shootings will be reduced." To carry out the study, 10 or 12 roads leading in and out of the worst gang neighborhood in Los Angeles were blocked with cement barriers. Drive-by shooting statistics were analyzed for two years both before and after the roads were blocked. Findings from the blocked neighborhood were compared to three other neighborhoods with demographics similar to those of the program neighborhood. Findings revealed that drive-by shootings between gang members were 70 percent lower in the blocked neighborhood compared to the neighborhoods that were not blocked.

10. F.B.I. AGENT STUDY

This study reports findings from personal interviews with 50 F.B.I. agents who have investigated terrorist activities in the United States. Based on the results of the interviews, the data collected from the agent sample suggest that terrorist activity in the United States is expected to increase in the next century. The main predictor of this trend, according to the interview data, is the increasing number of European terrorist groups establishing roots in major U.S. cities.

INDEX

E	A	A	D
U	C	A	B
E	serias	d	B
E	reporting	A	A
C	A	A	D
A	C	C	D
A	C	C	A
A	C	C	B
B	d	B	C
B	A	A	A
A	A	d	
A	d	A	
d	B	C	
d	⌐Ba	B	
A	25 ┤A?	C	
C	┤A?	C	
A	┤B?	B	
C	└AP	A	
C	d	C	
d	A	C	
A	C	B	
d	B	B	
C	C	d	
C	B	64 ⌐Deal g	
B	B	└Fallers	
22	A		
	A		
	A		
	A		
	46		